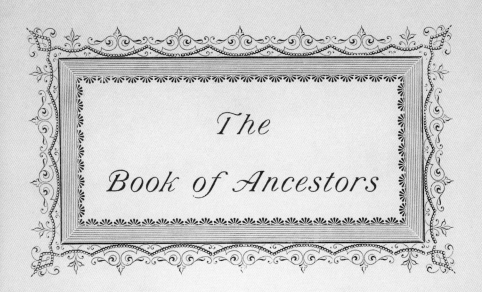

The
Book of Ancestors

ALSO BY CLAIRE GOODCHILD

The Book of Séances

The
Book
of
Ancestors

**A Guide to Magic, Rituals,
and Your Family History**

Claire Goodchild

VORACIOUS

Little, Brown and Company
New York Boston London

Voracious / Little, Brown and Company
Hachette Book Group
1290 Avenue of the Americas, New York, NY 10104
voraciousbooks.com

First Edition: October 2023

Voracious is an imprint of Little, Brown and Company, a division of Hachette Book Group, Inc. The Voracious name and logo are trademarks of Hachette Book Group, Inc.

The publisher is not responsible for websites (or their content) that are not owned by the publisher.

The Hachette Speakers Bureau provides a wide range of authors for speaking events. To find out more, go to hachettespeakersbureau.com or email hachettespeakers@hbgusa.com.

Little, Brown and Company books may be purchased in bulk for business, educational, or promotional use. For information, please contact your local bookseller or the Hachette Book Group Special Markets Department at special.markets@hbgusa.com.

Designed by Leah Carlson-Stanisic

ISBN 9780316353540
LCCN 2023931951

10 9 8 7 6 5 4 3 2 1

MOHN

Printed in Germany

For my ancestors (especially the Goodchilds):
Thank you for helping to guide my life even through death,
and for teaching me that we have value beyond our struggles.

The Poulis Portrait Studio

By opening this book, you have just taken your first deliberate step toward developing a spiritual relationship with your ancestors.

The truth is, you probably already participate in ancestor veneration (a term for honoring your ancestors), you just don't realize it.

I like to use the 1995 film *Clueless* as an example of how ancestor veneration often begins. Within the first ten minutes of the movie, the main character, Cher, holds a geometry test up to a portrait of her deceased mother and informs her of the good grade she earned.

This simple gesture is an act of working with ancestors.

Chances are you do little things for your ancestors, much like Cher. Maybe you toast your deceased grandparents during holiday meals, or ask your dad's spirit to watch over you before a big work presentation.

Ancestor work is the act of developing a spiritual relationship with the spirits of our deceased family and friends and turning it into a consistent practice.

Making your ancestors a part of your spiritual routine or practice can enrich your life in myriad ways. Not only can it provide you with answers to questions and help you connect to your own history, but your ancestors can also play a beneficial role in improving your life through magic and ritual.

Not everything we uncover or learn on this journey will be easy. Ancestor work requires dedication and consistency, but don't let this intimidate you. Like all magical or spiritual work, the more energy you put into it, the more you will get out of it.

You already possess the skill set needed to build these relationships with spirits—you just need the tools and direction to get started. My hope is that this book can be your guide in that process.

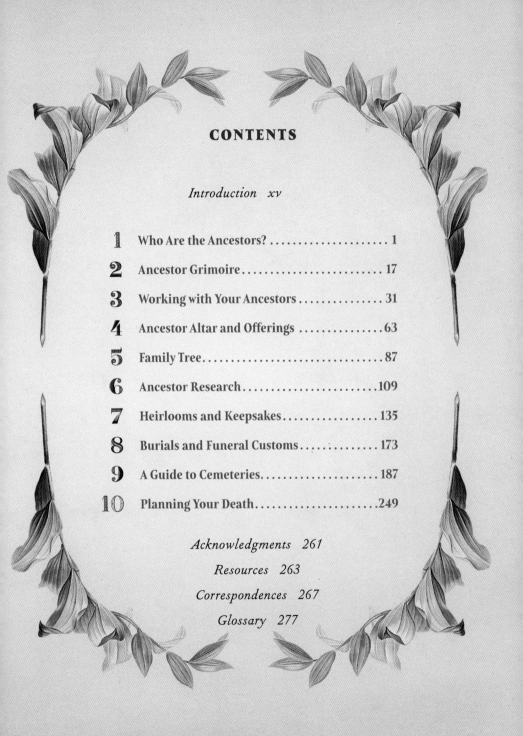

CONTENTS

Introduction xv

INTRODUCTION

A few short years ago, I was feeling lost and unsteady in my life. I was newly sober and struggling with what that meant for my identity.

You see, I didn't know who I was without alcohol. I knew who I wished I was, but I didn't think it was possible to get there. It was as if I had the destination, but no road map to follow.

Each day was a battle between my old self and this new *terrified* self. I had all these people around me telling me who I was, but none of their descriptors felt correct or comfortable.

One day, in a moment when I felt like giving up and caving in to my cravings, I closed my eyes and asked for a sign.

It was then that my sign appeared. Hundreds of them, actually. They came in the form of my ancestors. There in my mind's eye they stood. Rows and rows of them, spanning decades and centuries.

I had always felt my grandparents' spirits around me—and if you've read *The Book of Séances*, then you know I refer to the dead as my constant companions—but this felt different. It was an internal pull toward something. Something that was old and new all at once. It was a pull toward understanding legacy.

In this daydream or vision or whatever you want to call it, each of my ancestors held a different object in their hands. Objects I would later realize were headstone symbols—a language I have since learned is very useful for communicating with the spirits.

There was something else peculiar about this experience: one-quarter of these ancestors were frozen, unmoving. It was quite obvious to me that these frozen spirits were my paternal ancestors—particularly my paternal grandfather's line. The ones who struggled with addiction.

They say that the past informs the future, or at the very least the present. I realized that if I wanted to understand who I was and who I wanted to be, I needed to understand where I came from.

When I was growing up, not many positive stories were shared with me about my paternal ancestors. I had been indoctrinated to believe that their lives were nothing more than their addictions. And, as the one in the family who took after them in terms of my physical looks and personality traits, I believed that same lie about myself. This lie said that no matter what I accomplished, in the end, my struggles would be the only thing I was remembered for.

As an already-practicing witch who had an abundance of experience in spirit communication and paranormal investigating, I thought the transition to ancestor work would be easy, but boy was I wrong.

The four years following my journey into this realm were difficult. While there was an abundance of wonderful resources out there for the ritual aspect of ancestor work, they included very little on how to research and study genealogy. Without that factual foundation, I couldn't feel a connection to the magic I was being asked to perform. I realized that in order to do ancestor work, I would have to start with the data and learn to combine the two.

Another problem I faced was that each avenue of study or experiment led back to the same spiritual roadblock: that healing the ancestral trauma in my family was entirely up to me, and that it was the only worthwhile part of ancestor magic.

Thankfully, I realized early that this is an impossible task and not the be-all and end-all of this practice.

Don't get me wrong, trauma is covered in this book—after all, it is my trauma that originally sent me down this road. But making trauma the sole focus of ancestor work reinforces the idea that our trauma is the sum of our identities. And it's not. No one person can heal thousands of years of pain.

I wanted to know who my paternal ancestors were without alcohol. Who were they apart from their trauma? If I couldn't answer these questions about them, how could I possibly answer them about myself?

These questions forced me to explore other paths in the spirit world, ones I might not have otherwise followed. Headstones and their inscriptions revealed artistic taste, socioeconomic status, and religious beliefs. Locating old addresses and learning about the surrounding neighborhoods provided me with information on local flora and fauna to incorporate into rituals. Old shop names, advertisements, and even receipts offered a glimpse into my ancestors' daily habits and routines. Newspaper articles and court records revealed accomplishments as well as some periods of turmoil.

I learned that my ancestors were multifaceted and complex. They lived, loved, and sometimes suffered. Remembering them for only one negative aspect of their lives had not only held them back, but it had held me back as well.

By freeing my ancestors' memories from the confines of their faults, I ended up freeing myself from those same limiting beliefs. This quest taught me to be consistent and thoughtful in my exploration not only of my ancestors and other spirits, but, most importantly, of myself.

I feel incredibly lucky that I now have the opportunity to teach you everything I've learned during this process. My hope is that you too can uncover the people you are descended from, their stories, and the legacy you and your ancestors will leave behind.

As you move forward with this book, remember that we all have ancestral trauma, but ancestral trauma is not all we have.

WHO IS CLAIRE?

The short version of my story goes something like this: I'm Claire and I'm an artist and author who spends much of her time talking with ghosts.

The long version takes place over the last thirty-five years, as well as across the millennia in which my ancestors have lived and died.

In the interest of time, I will share with you the version that falls somewhere in the middle.

I have been a witch for two-thirds of my life. I found my spell-casting legs, like most millennial witches, on the Wiccan and pagan message boards of the early internet and in the pages of the few beginner books that were available at the library.

I was first introduced to the community when I was just eleven years old, by a family friend, and I took to witchcraft immediately. I was a sensitive and shy kid surrounded by chaos, and it was something I could focus on that made me feel confident.

Two years before this, I had been witness to my maternal grandfather's death. An event that contained too many unusual and otherworldly circumstances to be chalked up to mere coincidence. This experience led to my insatiable curiosity about ghosts and spirits.

Witchcraft provided answers about those things in a way that differed from the mainstream. Instead of telling me that the spirit realm was dangerous or "evil," the majority of these pagan spaces embraced death—in a respectful and compassionate way. Pagans used their personal beliefs to better themselves, their communities, and the afterlives of their ancestors.

Witchcraft taught me that energy doesn't end when something or someone has died. It just changes. That power or life-force (spirit) finds a new outlet or way to be expressed.

This made sense to me. After all, how could the afterlife automatically be someplace bad, or filled with dark forces whose sole purpose was to hurt people, if all of our loved ones were also there? Surely for every "negative entity" on the other side, there are one hundred positive ones looking out for us.

When I began my deep dive into divination—predominantly tarot reading—I was underwhelmed by the decks available on the market. While beautiful, none of them really explored the Underworld or themes relating to spirits. I realized that in order to have the type of tarot deck I wanted, I would have to create it. So I did. This is how the Antique Anatomy Tarot was born.

At the start of my ancestor journey, I began to experiment with crafting different tarot and oracle decks whose focus was on paranormal investigation and spirit communication. This led to the creation of my Memento Mori Oracle, a deck designed to bridge the gap between the living and the dead.

"Memento Mori" is a phrase found on many headstones, as well as in literature and art; it is Latin for "Remember that you will die." It sounds grim, but it's actually a message of positivity. It is a reminder to live your life to the best of your ability because it's the only one you get.

Ancestor work is another one of these reminders. While some things, like our birth, are out of our control, other things we *do* have a say in—such as our character and how we treat people. Every person matters and every person has a story to share, and we can honor that by being willing to listen.

ABOUT THIS BOOK

Though I have dedicated my life to understanding the spirit world, that doesn't automatically mean that I am better at this than you. All it means is that I have had more practice with it. And it is this practice that has granted me the opportunity to help get you started on this journey...on the right foot.

Working with spirits—particularly your ancestors—doesn't take any special abilities, or a divine gift from God. You don't even need to identify as a witch. It just takes dedication, curiosity, and a willingness to learn. The stories of your ancestors are stories of the dead, but they are also the story of you.

The dead are around us all the time. They live in us. They live in our hearts, in our minds, and even in our DNA.

Within this book is everything I have learned during my own ancestor practice over the last five years. I am gifting you my rituals, my genealogy research tips, and guides to building family trees and working within cemetery walls, as well as instructions for creating your own ancestor grimoire—a hybrid spell book and family history book.

However, the most important thing I can teach you is this: Your relationship with your ancestors is unique to you. Nothing I have written is set in (grave) stone. Take what I have shared and make it your own.

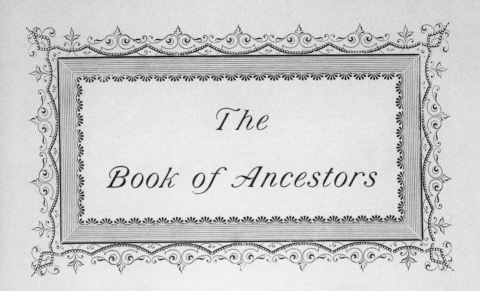

The

Book of Ancestors

CHAPTER ONE

WHO ARE THE ANCESTORS?

Who Are the Ancestors?

THE SPIRIT WORLD

We all die. It's an unfortunate reality for every living being on earth. Because our lives in the physical realm are limited, death will ultimately be the state in which we spend the majority of our existence. Because of this, we must become comfortable with death. And while death may separate us from our loved ones in a physical sense, death also unites us on a human scale because it is a common experience. When someone dies, we instinctively come together.

Being comfortable with death doesn't mean we need to be *happy* about death—I want that to be clear. Death has a profound impact on our lives. This doesn't mean we can't mourn or be angry about the loss of life. It just means we need to realize that dying is a transformative process from one state of being to another.

Working with your ancestors is about establishing a relationship with death and everything that comes along with it. This includes the spirits of your ancestors, as well as the spirits of other humans and of sacred areas belonging to the dead, such as graveyards.

We all have ancestors and we all can benefit from building a posthumous relationship with them.

You don't need to be a witch to start this process, nor do you need to have a concrete idea just yet about what ancestor work will provide for you. Chances are your ancestors are already watching over you and helping to guide your life. By taking on an active role in this relationship, you will improve and strengthen it.

> **DANGERS AND PRECAUTIONS:** Many people are nervous about beginning spirit work because they have been led to believe it is inherently dangerous. Frankly, this just isn't true.
>
> Of course, there are precautions that you should take to protect yourself (I cover those in depth in chapter 3), but it really comes down to common sense. The rules and boundaries you use to protect yourself from abusive or dangerous people in the living world are easily transferable to the spirit world. Just as the majority of people you interact with in our world are kind and courteous, the same can be said about the spirits of the dead.

SPIRITS

A spirit is the animating force of a living thing. This applies not just to people, but to all things on earth. I am of the belief that the spirit of a person continues to exist in some form even after death—it just no longer animates a physical body. The spirit is also sometimes referred to as the soul.

GHOSTS

A ghost is the physical manifestation of a deceased person. This manifestation is known as an apparition. The conscious spirit of the deceased isn't always present with their ghost form when it manifests.

> The terms "ghost" and "spirit" are often used interchangeably, and this is fine.

HAUNTINGS

Hauntings are interactions between a spirit or ghost and the living world. There are two main categories of hauntings you should understand: intelligent hauntings and residual hauntings.

Intelligent hauntings are when the spirit or ghost is aware of their interaction with the living world. With intelligent hauntings, the manifestation and interaction are often deliberate. When a spirit leaves a message or sign, that is an intelligent haunting. When you participate in activities such as divination in order to communicate with a spirit, you are taking part in an intelligent haunting.

Residual hauntings are instances in which a ghost manifests without consciously doing so. These are usually energetic imprints left on an environment that replay on a loop, such as an apparition walking up a flight of stairs. Residual hauntings generally don't include the consciousness of the deceased. It's as if a small portion of the spirit was left behind or got stuck in some fashion. They are not choosing to be there and are not aware of it.

THE SPIRIT REALM OR THE OTHER SIDE

"The spirit realm" and "the other side" are catchall terms for the place the spirit goes upon death. There are countless beliefs about what this place is or may be. For some it is called heaven, while for others it is a place that mirrors the living world. Others believe that the living realm and the spirit realm are on the same plane of existence—the living just can't always see the spirit side.

> Take a few moments and think about what "the other side" means to you. What do you imagine it is like? Has religion or your personal spiritual belief shaped your ideas?

ANCESTORS

Ancestors are the people whom we are descended from in either a literal sense (through genetics) or a spiritual sense (such as through mentors).

There are three types of ancestors you will learn about in this book: blood ancestors, community ancestors, and archetype ancestors.

Blood ancestors

Your blood ancestors are those whom you are related to genetically. Because these ancestors will be the main focus of this book (as well as of your ancestor practice), we don't need to go into too much detail now, but here are the basics.

> **Note on adoption and stepparents:** I include adoptive relatives and stepparents in blood ancestor work. If you are adopted or have a stepfamily, please feel free to use the terms that work best for you. I have one friend who refers to her adoptive family as her soul family and her genetic family as her birth family.

Your blood ancestors include your parents, your parents' parents, and so on all the way back to the beginning of our species.

When starting an ancestor practice, I recommend working only with your parental lineage up to five or six generations back, so you don't get overwhelmed. Bear in mind that when you reach back six generations, you are looking at sixty-four different fourth great-grandparents!

An easy way to determine how many grandparents are in each generation is by doubling the number of parents.

For example:

- You have two biological parents.
- They each have two biological parents, which brings you to four grandparents.
- Those four grandparents each have two parents, so that brings you to eight great-grandparents.

As you can see, the relatives add up quickly, which can lead to mistakes and other issues when doing your research. You'll also be spread so thin that each an-

The Oldfield Art Studio
TORONTO · LONDON · NEW YORK

cestor may not get the attention they deserve. Not to mention how these issues multiply when dealing with adoptive relatives and stepfamily or in-laws!

Of course, all families are unique. If you want to work with ancestors such as aunts, uncles, and cousins, please do. You know better than I do who should be included as you begin your practice. **Always listen to your instincts.**

While we are on this topic, it's important to know that you also have the right to *not* work with any ancestor you choose. If someone was abusive or did unforgivable things, they do not need to be included. This also means that just because you do choose to work with these people, you are not necessarily condoning or agreeing with their behavior. This is a deeply personal experience, and nobody can tell you what is best for you.

Connecting with your blood ancestors

For right now, if you have never worked with your blood ancestors before, all you need to do to initiate contact with these spirits is to take a moment to introduce yourself out loud and let them know you will be in touch again soon.

Over the days that follow, you may start to notice odd little occurrences around you: like seeing shadows out of the corner of your eye, or maybe smelling perfume, or even dreaming about people you've never met before.

You don't need to do anything about it yet, just observe and take notes if you wish.

Community ancestors

Community ancestors are those whom we connect with on an identity level. We're all born into various communities, such as social identity groups like the LGBTQ2S community, or cultural communities, such as Latvians or Congolese. Other communities we are part of by choice, through, say, our religious affiliations and our vocations.

Working with community ancestors can be a very rewarding experience. It can be beneficial to give thanks to those who opened doors for us as well as for future generations.

When it comes to working with community ancestors, there are some guidelines I believe should be followed.

The first is that you should ask them only for protection.

While I believe that our blood ancestors can be called upon for a variety of reasons, and that we can have higher expectations of their involvement, we shouldn't place that same burden on community ancestors.

For one, our relationship with community ancestors is not as personal, and the focus of our work with these groups should be to the benefit of the wider community we're all part of and not just ourselves.

Protection is a good thing to ask for because it is something all community members can share.

The second thing I believe should be the focus of your community ancestor work is making time to give thanks.

Giving thanks to those who helped pave the way for us isn't just about saying thank you (though that is always appreciated), it is also about giving back. This is known as an act of service.

Throughout this book, you will see different types of acts of service. These are actions we take in order to help our community, to give back to our ancestors, *and* to say thank you.

In witchcraft, it is imperative to not only engage in the act of taking. You must also be willing to give.

Connecting with your community ancestors

A good way to start connecting with and honoring your community ancestors is by making a monetary donation of some sort. If you are a woman or femme-identifying person who works in STEM, helping to pay for science camp for a young girl not only helps the next generation, but also gives thanks to the women who opened the door for you.

Of course, not all acts of service need to be monetary. Volunteering one's time and lending one's hand to community projects are also admirable actions.

In order to begin your relationship with these spirits, take some time to write down which community ancestors you feel drawn to, as well as ideas you have about how you might thank them.

Archetype ancestors

The archetype ancestors are a special group because they can be the spirits of individual people, but they also exist as an independent energy or idea.

An archetype is a universal model or group of characteristics and concepts. These concepts are what influence human behavior.

Archetypes exist across all cultures throughout time and appear in literature, folklore, art, and religion...though most people associate the idea of archetypes with Swiss psychologist Carl Jung. But Jung didn't create archetypes, he just gave certain ones names and categories.

Archetypes represent the human experience. They can symbolize our motivations and explain how these motivations are expressed through personality traits.

In a spiritual sense, archetypal energy is neither inherently good nor inherently bad, it just exists. It is our underlying motivations that determine which way each archetype swings: positive or negative.

Both your main ancestors, blood, and your secondary ancestors, community, can be grouped into the archetypal categories.

Not only can we learn a lot about our ancestors through archetypes, but we can also become better acquainted with ourselves. We all contain a blend of every archetypal energy that exists (there are hundreds, maybe even thousands) but often feel more connected with one than with the others.

Archetypes can also be worked with on their own. Remember what I said earlier about archetypes also existing as independent energy. Archetypal work can be useful if you don't yet feel ready to work with your blood or community ancestors.

Below you will find the five main archetypes I work with in my practice. Though there are countless different archetypes in existence, I think starting with only a few will help you to get acquainted with the concept. Some of my archetypes you may recognize, others you may not. You may find that my categories do not suit your needs, and I encourage you to adjust them or even create your own!

I also recommend studying Jung's twelve archetypes and seeing if any of those speak to you.

The forgotten

The forgotten are those who have been lost or hidden over the centuries. This obscuration could be deliberate, or be the result of the passage of time. Some ancestors are shunned or erased purposefully as punishment for their actions, while others—such as illegitimate children—were never included in the family to begin with and are innocent victims of omission. In some cases, these ancestors being forgotten is unintentional: people just stopped talking about them.

Identifying the forgotten

* Babies and children who died young
* Shunned ancestors
* Out-of-wedlock or secret children
* Victims of genocide
* People of lost or erased civilizations and communities

We all have forgotten ancestors. Even if their names and stories cannot be told with intimate detail, they should still be acknowledged. The forgotten ancestors need us in a way that the others don't. They rely on us to be revived and remembered.

The protectors

Protection comes in many different forms. It can be brash and obvious, like a warrior defending their land from invaders, or it can be subtle and gentle, like a child taking their younger sibling outside so they won't hear their parents fighting.

Those who fall into the protector archetype group are those who are hyper-aware of danger. Sometimes these dangers are real threats, and other times they are imagined threats born of trauma.

When it comes to spirits of the dead, most protectors were forced into the role based on what they experienced during their lifetime, but some just have a natural affinity for safeguarding others.

Identifying the protectors

* Warriors and community leaders
* Parents and older children
* Land defenders
* Firefighters and other first responders, as well as social workers

The protectors can be called upon for protection rituals and act as middlemen between us and other ancestors and spirits—especially when we're just starting out on this journey. It is imperative that we also encourage this archetype to rest. They spend much of their time in the spirit world looking out for others, and therefore we need to look out for them in return.

The teachers

The teachers are the archetype that provides advice and presides over all matters relating to communication. It is these ancestors whom you may actually notice first when you begin your ancestor journey.

Teachers come in many different forms. Parents and grandparents are often our first teachers, so by default these people can be included in this category; however, only a select few will end up staying in this archetype as you move further along in your practice.

The members of this archetype provide us with the guidance and skills we need to lead successful lives. Unfortunately, they don't always teach us "healthy" skills and behaviors. This is as true in death as it is in life. Some of your ancestors will be wonderful teachers and thrive in this archetype, while others will fail spectacularly at it.

Identifying the teachers

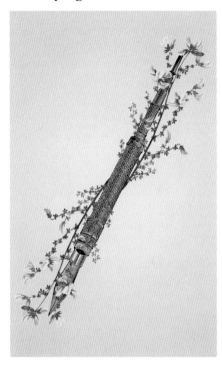

* Schoolteachers and historians
* Religious leaders and elders
* Parents and grandparents
* Tradespeople
* Writers and journalists

The teacher archetypes are wonderful to call on when it comes to actively researching your ancestry. They help us to uncover secrets and explore ideas from a variety of different angles. However, the teachers should also be reminded that not everything needs to have a lesson attached to it. Some things can be just for fun.

The reapers

The reaper archetype sounds a lot scarier than it actually is. You will want to think of these spirits as the welcoming committee for new arrivals. Good, bad, right, and wrong are irrelevant to these spirits. Their job is to keep things in balance and in order.

Surprisingly, their job is also to provide comfort to other spirits and help guide them through the transition from their life to their new reality in death. Comfort doesn't always equal coddling or acting in an overly nurturing way; sometimes it is just about providing structure and stability when it's needed most.

Identifying the reapers

* Judges and other public servants
* Doctors, midwives, and death doulas
* Undertakers and funeral directors

The reapers are the ones to call when you need to make tough decisions or are going through a major change in your life. As with the Death card in tarot (which features a reaper), the reaper doesn't always speak of physical death, but often represents a *symbolic death* of something that no longer serves our spirit. The reapers are the archetypes who show us what we have outgrown.

The thread spinners

The thread spinners are the archetype that stands out from the others. They have a quiet authority, almost like they command attention without trying. I think we all have that type of person in our lives: the ones who perhaps aren't the most beautiful or the most intelligent or the wealthiest, but who have a magnetism that attracts others. People listen to and respect them.

Identifying the thread spinners

* The driving force in a family
* The thread that holds everyone together

Like the reapers, the thread spinners come around most during difficult or life-changing events. Whereas the reapers teach us to accept things as they are, the thread spinners offer us solutions and creative ways to alter our situations. If you don't like the fabric of your life, they show you how to cut it apart and start sewing something new.

In many cultures, the thread spinners are known as fate or destiny figures. Fate isn't about things being completely set in stone, with no free will or agency. Fate changes based on the decisions you make, and what decisions others make that affect you.

Think of your life as one long thread with you holding one end and a thread spinner holding the other in the spirit world. At times this thread can get knotted, and we need help to untangle it. It's then that we tend to feel this archetype most, as if a higher power has stepped in to help us. This is what's known as a spirit guide.

A spirit guide is the special entity or ancestor who spends the most time with us of all our ancestors. They do this by choice, and it is to make sure we have as few tangles as possible in our thread. These spirit guides, known as guardian angels to some, interact with us more than other spirits. They generally don't wait to be called on for help and will just show up.

Honoring the archetypes

In chapter 3, I teach you a daily candle ritual to perform for your ancestors. The archetypes can also be included in this practice. Additionally, there is a color correspondence list at the back of the book that can help you identify which colors may be beneficial to incorporate into your rituals.

The forgotten
    Candle color: gold or purple
    Time: once a week, month, or year

The protectors
    Candle color: black, green, or orange
    Time: once a month or on a special holiday such as a Sabbat, birthday, or death day

The teachers
    Candle color: yellow or blue
    Time: once a month or on a special holiday such as a Sabbat, birthday, or death day

The reapers
    Candle color: brown or pink
    Time: once a month or on a special holiday such as a Sabbat, birthday, or death day

The thread spinners
    Candle color: red
    Time: once a month or on a special holiday such as a Sabbat, birthday, or death day

CHAPTER TWO

ANCESTOR GRIMOIRE

Ancestor Grimoire

It's human nature to want to leave your mark on the world; to leave something that says, "I was here."

The first humans did this through art and other symbolic markings. Our earliest ancestors drew on cave walls with red ochre pigments and carved images into the rocky surface as a way of sharing an experience with future generations.

These ancient images were how they told their stories: stories about magic and rituals, the ins and outs of daily life; these images also served as maps of geographical areas, as markers of territory.

How many of us have done something similar? Carved our name into a park bench or marked a bathroom stall with a funny quip or anecdote?

Everything is communicated through symbols. Symbols are how we express our thoughts, feelings, and desires in a succinct and direct way.

Words are just another form of symbol. If I show you the word "rose" and then a picture of a rose, you know what both of those mean. You can identify the rose and understand what I am sharing with you.

Language has always existed, whether through oral or symbolic traditions, but writing as we know it is an extremely modern concept.

Writing in a script form arrived somewhere between 3500 and 3000 BCE in Sumer, the southern region of the ancient civilization Mesopotamia.

This early writing is called cuneiform and was created by carving words into wet clay tablets.

Writing was first used to record the trade of specific items such as beer or livestock, but eventually evolved to include other subjects like religious ideas, mythology, and, of course, history.

LEAVING YOUR MARK

In this chapter, I will be covering the creation of a special ancestor book, a combination of a family history book and a magical grimoire. It will be your companion through the process of building your ancestor practice, and will be where you keep everything important relating to your journey.

Each chapter in *The Book of Ancestors* will provide you with content for your grimoire, which will be a combination of items you collect and entries you create. This book will be something you refer to frequently. As your ancestor practice grows, so will your book.

WHAT IS A FAMILY HISTORY BOOK?

A family history book is just what it sounds like: a collection of historical facts about your family. Family history books are a way to preserve the details and stories of a family line.

Motivations for creating one vary. For some, a family history is simply a way to honor their ancestors. Others may be the last of their lineage and want to ensure that their story is told. There's no wrong reason to write your family history, and unless you come from a famous group of people, chances are nobody will go out of their way to tell the story for you.

There are a variety of types of family history books.

- Some contain photos.
- Some are a written narrative telling a specific story or event.
- Some focus on only one ancestor or branch of the family.

- And some are like scrapbooks containing whatever information, records, and stories are available.

It's this last type that we will be combining with our grimoire.

WHAT IS A GRIMOIRE?

Grimoires and spell books are like magical cookbooks. They provide a person with recipes for crafting different spells and charms.

Grimoires also contain a blend of a person's belief systems, personal mythology, local or familial customs, and symbols (such as what different plants or animals represent), as well as individual history and experiences.

You will find a dictionary of symbols commonly found on headstones in chapter 9.

As with family history books, some people have different grimoires for different areas of study, such as astrology or plants.

It can be argued that *all* religious texts, from those early clay tablets to the hundred-pound Bibles found in churches, are grimoires, but the ones we associate with the word first appeared in the medieval and early modern periods, thanks to Johannes Gutenberg's invention of the printing press. These books were used to share knowledge about alchemy, protection, and even medicine.

In the nineteenth and twentieth centuries, when séances and spiritualism became the rage, grimoires were brought back into the spotlight. Hundreds of books, leaflets, and pamphlets were published on the secrets of the universe and how to communicate with spirits.

In some branches of witchcraft—particularly Wicca—the grimoire is called a Book of Shadows. Though this term is most often used in the Wiccan religion, all sorts of different pagans and witches use the term "Book of Shadows," or BOS for short.

CREATING YOUR FAMILY GRIMOIRE

As I said earlier, we will be creating a grimoire–family history hybrid of sorts.

This book will be a combination of facts and history about your ancestors, as well as any magical workings (spells and rituals) you then perform using these facts.

NAMING YOUR GRIMOIRE

What you call your grimoire is completely up to you. Some people like the term "ancestor grimoire," others like "family grimoire" or "family spell book." I call mine my personal Book of Ancestors, or BOA for short. This is an homage to the term "Book of Shadows," because even though I am not a Wiccan, it was the Wiccan faith that first brought me into the witchcraft community.

"BOA" will be used to refer to your family grimoire throughout the rest of this book.

HARD COPY OR DIGITAL

There are two routes you can go when it comes to crafting your BOA: hard copy or digital.

I recommend creating a hard-copy book. Having something you can physically hold can help you feel connected to your ancestors, and my instructions throughout this book are most relevant to a physical BOA.

However, there are pros to having a digital BOA, such as backup (later in this book, I recommend you digitize every single record you come across). If you're doing this, it is pretty easy to compile your records into a virtual book or PDF.

Not only that, but a digital BOA is also safe from physical damage (provided it's properly backed up). It is also very easy to organize and reorganize.

MATERIAL

When it comes to crafting your BOA, it's best to choose something like a three-ring binder or journal that can be altered to fit extra pages.

I have four main grimoires: one for each of my grandparents and their family lines. Each one is housed in a leather binder so that as my knowledge about my family and practice grows, I can expand the books.

Take your time choosing the appropriate home for your BOA. If you can't decide what to use, begin by just getting a file folder or small binder to collect any information you already have.

ORGANIZING YOUR GRIMOIRE

There are three ways you can organize your BOA: by topic, by ancestor, and by a mixture of the two. I find the third option to be the best, as it allows you to cover all your bases. Everything you learn about your ancestors should be put into this book.

Below are some of my recommended categories. These sections are for your blood ancestors, but you can also assign a section for your community ancestors and your archetype ancestors, as there will be overlap among all three groups. Feel free to adjust as needed.

- Book blessing
- Family trees, family crests, and other emblems
- Name meanings

Harvey Powell

der: Male

Date: June 25th 1868

Birth Place: Lincolnshire, England

: Eliza Powell (née Lucsby)

Death Date: April 7th 1913

Death Place: Toronto, Ontario, Canada

Cemetery: Prospect Cemetery

Burial: Toronto, Ontario, Canada

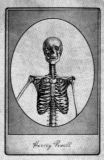

Harvey Powell

Photo taken in 1895
Lincolnshire.
Photographer: unknown

PROSPECT CEMETERY.

- Marriage records
- Church records
- Cemetery and burial records
- Funeral records
- Neighborhood and country maps
- Lore and mythology (by region)
- Family legends and folktales
- Census records
- Photographs
- Recipes
- Heirlooms
- Spells and rituals
- Records of offerings
- Divination records
- Individual ancestor profiles

Example of a category and its contents:

Cemetery section: *Death and burial records, maps, plot numbers and ownership records, headstone symbols and descriptions, offerings, and cemetery history*

Set aside a few pages in the back of your BOA for an activity we will be working on in chapter 10, "Planning Your Death."

BOOK BLESSING

Your BOA is a sacred object, and you should treat it as such.

No matter whether you have chosen a custom leather-embossed journal or a simple notebook to be your BOA, the volume needs to be properly taken care of. This means keeping it free from dirt and debris, and finding an appropriate home for it—preferably somewhere near your ancestor altar (chapter 4).

You also need to perform a book blessing on it.

The purpose of a book blessing is protection. You want not only yourself but also your environment to be spiritually safe and looked after.

Performing the book blessing

Before you begin, you must understand that this process will not be completed in a day. Building a relationship with your ancestors is a marathon, not a sprint, and creating your book is no exception.

Cleansing

The first step of the blessing is to cleanse your book. You will want to remove the energy left behind by everyone who handled it before it was in your possession.

One of my favorite processes for this sort of purification is smoke cleansing. I find the juniper plant to be particularly good at this job. If you can forage and dry your own, that is great, but if not, juniper incense can work instead.

What you need

- A dried branch of juniper
- A fireproof dish to catch ashes
- Your BOA
- Matches or a lighter

Light the juniper and pass your BOA through the smoke a total of three times.

> If this method isn't possible, check out the cleansing methods for haunted objects on pages 170-71 and see if any of those might be viable.

Congratulations: Your book is now ready to be blessed—easy, right?

To perform the blessing portion of this ritual, you will need two special items: ritual ink and an ancestor sigil.

Ritual ink

To make your ritual ink, you will need one bottle of black scribe's ink (fountain pen or dip pen ink of the sort that can be found at a stationery store) and dried petals from a flower that means something to you.

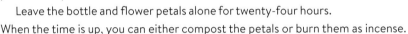

Place the bottle where it will not be disturbed and then sprinkle the flower petals around the bottle. As you do this, envision both yourself and your book being protected by centuries of ancestors.

Leave the bottle and flower petals alone for twenty-four hours. When the time is up, you can either compost the petals or burn them as incense.

Additional steps

If you'd like to give your ink a bit of spiritual "oomph," you can add one drop of blood from your finger. This is completely optional, and you should always use a sterile medical lancet to draw the blood.

If you're as squeamish as I am, you can take a few drops of red ink and mix it into your black ritual ink. This acts as symbolic blood.

Another way to add a little extra power to your ritual ink is by using a special resin-based ink. Many pagan and metaphysical stores carry these pigments, so they are easy to track down. One of the most popular types is dragon's blood ink, a bright red resin made from plants, which makes a great ritual ink for ancestor work due to its spiritually protective properties.

Ancestor sigil

The next step in the book blessing process is to create a special ancestor sigil.

A sigil is a magical symbol. This symbol contains a desire or intent for something—in this case, that intent is blessing and protection.

Your sigil should contain two elements: an image that represents protection and an image that represents your ancestors.

These symbols are then merged to form one image.

Creating a sigil can be intimidating, especially if you are new to this sort of thing, but I still highly recommend giving it a try.

To decide on the "protection" portion of the sigil, think of what protection means to you. What does that look like? For some, it's a knight's shield; for others, it could be a rock or a plant. Try not to overthink this step; whatever comes to mind is probably what you should use. You can also think back to a time when you felt protected by your ancestors in a way you couldn't quite explain. What symbol would you give that experience?

If you're still having trouble deciding, you can flip to the headstone symbols dictionary on pages 227–43 and see if anything speaks to you.

When it comes to settling on a symbol that represents your ancestors, nobody can decide for you. Some of you may have the answer immediately, while others may take more time. If you're really stuck, pick one ancestor you were close with and incorporate their name or initials into the design.

Next you will put the two symbols together and create an aesthetically pleasing design. This can be as abstract or realistic as you'd like.

Once your design is ready, flip to the very first page of your BOA and draw your sigil in the center with your ritual ink.

Your book is now blessed.

> **TIP:** If you find this exercise extremely challenging, write the words "protection" and "ancestors" in the center of the page with your ritual ink. You can always revisit this another time as you gain more knowledge and experience with the spirits.

SPELLS AND RITUALS

I have mentioned that your BOA will also house your spells and rituals, but what are those exactly?

What is a spell?

A spell is essentially a word or phrase that is either spoken or written to grant the caster a desired outcome.

What is a ritual?

A ritual is a series of actions that can include spells, movements, or other actions that either honor an occurrence or invoke some desired outcome.

> These terms are often used interchangeably (this book is no exception).

When someone begins a spiritual or magical practice, they often copy a spell or ritual exactly. This is perfectly fine because it teaches you *how* to perform a spell or ritual, but it doesn't work exactly the same way with ancestor magic, because ancestor magic is highly personal.

Now of course, if you are a beginner, I advise you to copy my rituals as exactly as you need to until you feel comfortable branching out on your own. Think of mine as a jumping-off point. Little by little, you can start tweaking things to match your beliefs and your knowledge.

When performing an ancestor ritual for an individual or a group of ancestors, you should always consider the following:

Nationalities and countries lived in: This can help you find local lore and customs pertaining to your ancestors.

Time period lived in: Again, different customs can be more popular in certain periods than others.

Professions: For many people, work is how they spend the majority of their time. Understanding someone's occupation can give you insight into their daily life.

Favorite foods and colors: If you are lucky enough to know these things, USE THEM.

Example

I like to communicate with my paternal grandmother via tea-leaf reading. I can use any old cup and tea and probably get a decent response, or I can make sure this ritual is tailored to her in order to get the best possible response.

So what do I do?

Well, to start, I use one of the teacups I inherited from her collection. Then I choose an English tea to honor her heritage.

Now, I can stop there, or I can take the personalization even further by decorating my ancestor altar (chapter 4) with roses, which are her favorite flower, and in the background I can turn on some big-band jazz music, her favorite style.

The same ingredients can be used in other spells and rituals. Let's say I want to ask my grandmother to support me in a job interview. I take some classic "finance and career" spell ingredients, such as a green candle and patchouli, and then blend them with offerings for my grandmother, such as anointing the candle with rose oil and sprinkling English tea leaves on my altar.

By including ingredients I associate with my grandmother in the spell, I not only create a more inviting environment for her spirit, but I also show my willingness to reciprocate when asking for her help, and the respect I have for her input.

CHAPTER THREE

WORKING WITH YOUR ANCESTORS

3

Working with Your Ancestors

The first step in beginning your ancestor practice is figuring out your *why*.

Why do you want to honor and work with your ancestors?
What do you hope this practice will provide for you?

Remember: There is no one right answer to this question. Your why and my why could look completely different.

Assign a page to your why in your BOA so you can revisit it as your practice grows. You may find that your why changes over time, or that your whys contradict one another...this is fine.

> TIP: If you are using a bound notebook or journal for your BOA, be sure to leave a few extra pages at the beginning and end in case you need to make changes.

You'll be continually reminded throughout this journey that human beings are multifaceted and that different things can be true for a person at the same time.

It doesn't matter if you don't know yet exactly why you're interested in this path. Perhaps you just had a feeling that you should experiment, or you're simply curious about the process. Any reason at all is reason enough to try.

My whys

To understand my culture and ethnicity better
To learn who I am
To find where I fit in with my family
To help heal familial alcohol addiction
To have help and support from the spirit world in order to reach my goals
And finally…just because I want to

Now, as I mention in the discussion about protecting yourself later in this chapter, the relationship you have with your ancestors is a two-way street. It is imperative that you offer them something in return. This is what I call showing up for spirits, or showing up for your ancestors.

Imagine for a second how it would feel if you had a relative or friend who only came to you when they needed something. It wouldn't feel awesome, would it? Well, the same goes for your ancestors. They deserve more than to have you just fluttering in and out asking for things.

Yes, it is in their best interests that you do well in life because you are their legacy, but that doesn't give you the right to be selfish and inconsiderate.

Underneath your list of whys, you should write a second list called "What I can offer."

In this list you will record what it is you aim to provide to your ancestors in exchange for their help.

This is essentially a contract, but if you find that you're struggling to maintain the terms, you can modify it. Your ancestors are generally reasonable; they know life will sometimes pull you away or that you may go through periods when you can't keep up with everything.

Here's what I came up with for my own list.

What I can offer

That I will perform a candle ritual in their honor on my altar every day

That I will do ten to twenty minutes of divination every day

That I will do twenty minutes of research on their lives every day

That I will live well (more on this in a minute)

That I will include them in activities

That I will maintain and protect their burial spaces

Case-by-case basis: That I will share my ancestors' stories with the public and incorporate parts of their identities into my art and writing

As you can see, I have a pretty hefty list in my ancestor contract. I have been doing this work a long time, and I can keep up with these demands. If you're just starting out, try listing one or two things you know you can stick to.

DAILY CANDLE RITUAL

While I cover offerings more in the discussion about ancestor altars in chapter 4, I want to pass on my daily candle ritual to you here, so you have something you can get started on right away.

What you need

* One candle for each day (any color you want)
* A lighter or matches
* Something to carve with
* Ancestors

How to perform the ritual

First you need to record all the death anniversaries of the blood and community ancestors that you plan on working with. If you are unsure of a death day for a specific person, choose a day at random for now (a Sabbat also makes a good substitute—see pages 273–75). This of course applies to your ancient ancestors, whose death days will never be accessible to you.

Every day, at the same time, light a candle for your ancestors and let it burn through.

I use a new candle every single day and this part of the ritual takes me about two hours.

I can appreciate that not everyone has the budget or the time to do this.

If this is the case, what you can do instead is get one large candle and burn it for a few minutes at the same time every day.

Now, on a death day for one of my ancestors, the ritual is tailored to them entirely. I take a new candle, like I do every day, but this time I carve their name into the side of it and say the words "[Ancestor Name], I promise that as long as I am here on this earth, I will honor you to the best of my ability."

Then I spend a few minutes with my oracle deck and ask them if they have any messages they'd like to share. Those cards are then recorded in my BOA.

While your everyday candle can be used repeatedly, make sure on someone's death day that you give them their own candle and you find the time to burn it completely through.

If you are consistent with your ancestors, they will be consistent with you. Even though they are part of your spiritual team, they are not personal servants at your beck and call. By showing them respect through your consistent attention, you will find that your relationship grows, strengthens, and even heals.

In chapter 1, I noted different candle colors for each of the archetypes, if you would like to include any of them in your ritual.

PROTECTING YOURSELF

When it comes to spiritual work with the dead, there is one thing you cannot overlook: self-protection.

Self-protection is how you keep yourself emotionally, spiritually, and physically safe.

Television shows and online message boards, as well as some religious dogmata, have led people to believe that this work is inherently dangerous, but while negative things can (and have) happened, those situations are exceedingly rare.

However, we still need to make sure we are protected when engaging in spirit work. Just as abusive people exist in life, they can also exist in death.

LAYERS

Protection should be done in what I like to refer to as layers.

Layers are when you have multiple types of protection going at once, so that you are covered from all angles.

Whenever I am explaining this idea, I like to use the "home" analogy.

Your home is your space. You decide who is allowed in, and who is not.

The door to your home is a method of protection. It is your first layer. A closed door tells a person that permission is required to enter this space.

Unfortunately, not everyone respects closed doors. So in order to make sure you can keep them out, you add a lock. That is your second layer of protection.

A lock is enough to deter most people, but just in case it isn't, an alarm system or a security camera adds even more security.

Now you have three layers that warn people they should think twice about targeting your home.

Just like these layers protect you and your home from the living, the same idea can be applied to working with the dead.

When you grant someone permission to enter your home, there is a set of expectations about how that person should behave. There are cultural expectations that we all understand, such as not snooping in someone's belongings, and then there are expectations that you yourself set, such as not wanting someone to enter a specific room.

These expectations are your boundaries.

BOUNDARIES

The most important part of engaging in any form of spirit work—whether ancestor magic or paranormal investigating—is understanding boundaries.

Just as you might tell a living person that a room in your home is off-limits, you need to be able to do the same for the dead.

Most negative experiences result from beginners going into their spirit work without having any idea of what they want or need from the relationship.

Ancestor work is a partnership between you and the other side, which means there should be a reciprocal give-and-take.

The first step in figuring out what your boundaries are is to outline your list of rules. These rules should cover who can interact with you, how they can reach out to you, and when it is appropriate to work with you.

WHO CAN INTERACT WITH YOU

Deciding which spirits you work with is entirely up to you. For many, this is a baffling notion, because our lives have often revolved around not having any say in familial relationships.

In ancestor work you have agency, and there is nothing more powerful than that.

By establishing who is welcome in your house up front, you are setting a boundary as well as honoring the ancestors who didn't have a voice or the ability to make their own decisions—and this includes younger or previous versions of yourself.

Using myself as an example—I have established an open-door policy. Any of my ancestors are welcome to participate, but with the caveat that I can revoke their invitation at any time.

For instance, if you know right away that your grandmother Sue is going to overstep and railroad her way through your life, you can tell her right off the bat she is not invited to participate. There can be a lot of guilt surrounding boundaries, so just remind yourself that your health and happiness come first.

If you decide later on that you're secure enough to work with the aggressive spirit, you can take that step in your practice and invite them in.

HOW TO REACH YOU

When it comes to communicating with ancestors and spirits, everyone has a method they prefer. The most popular, of course, is divination, such as tarot reading or automatic writing.

Divination is fantastic for ancestor work because it is something anybody can learn, and there is a wide range of tools that can be used for this purpose.

Other methods that your ancestors may use to communicate with you include dreams, meditation, signs sent through objects, or perhaps even an internal dialogue.

By establishing how you'd prefer your ancestors to communicate with you, you're setting a boundary that prevents you from being caught off guard. You should understand, though, that for urgent matters they may reach out however they can.

WHEN THEY CAN WORK WITH YOU

This next boundary should be your strictest.

Deciding when you want to communicate with your ancestors is something that needs to be tailored to your lifestyle.

There will always be times when you are available to communicate and when you are not, and times when your ancestors can visit and when they cannot.

In *The Book of Séances*, I explain that whenever I pick up my tarot cards or I am at my altar, my ancestors have permission to come hang out. Outside of those two scenarios, I invite them on a case-by-case basis.

For instance, I may wake up in the morning and decide the whole day is open for any of them to visit. Other times, I may invite only certain people, or tailor the invitation to specific locations, like when I am at the cemetery for a few hours—which is technically when I am *their* guest.

One thing that I enforce pretty heavily is my no-intimacy policy.

Basically, if I am doing something that I wouldn't want any living relatives to see, I don't want the dead relatives to see it, either.

GROUNDING

The next layer of protection you'll want to soundly understand is grounding.

To be grounded is to feel secure, calm, and in control of the situation.

Like most aspects of this work, grounding looks different for everybody. As for me, I am most comfortable and clearheaded in the early morning or after I've done some sort of cardio workout. Other people are night owls who feel that same calm after tea and television.

EXTERNAL PROTECTION

Once we have done what we can to protect ourselves internally, it is time to look at external protection.

In other words, you can bring in physical objects that act as additional layers of protection.

Later in this book you will find additional protective amulets and talismans you can make for your home, but I want to provide an idea here to start you off.

Witch balls

Witch balls, or witches' balls, are glass ornaments filled with specific items that hang in windows or above doors of a home for the purpose of protection.

There are two main types of witch balls that you can make. The first is geared toward attracting positive energy in the home. The second type of witch ball is a trap for negative energy and spirits.

What you need

Two fillable glass ornaments—can be found at most craft stores or online

Dried chamomile, lavender, and rosemary

Various pieces of thread or string, pins, and nails

The first energy ornament we will be making is the positive one.

Take the cap off one ornament and fill it halfway with a combination of your dried herbs.

If you'd like to have more calming energy, you might consider adding a little extra chamomile. If you want the ball to be on the more protective side, you can add a little more rosemary. Lavender then brings the other two herbs together, as it is great for grounding.

Place the cap back on your ornament and hang it by your front door.

For the dark-energy ornament, you want to fill your ball with things that catch (thread or string) or harm (pins and nails).

Take the cap off the second ornament and fill it halfway with different lengths of thread or string.

You will want to twist and tangle these threads up so they look like a mess. They work as a "spiritual net" that catches negativity.

If you'd like to, you can add a few pins and nails to the ball as well. These represent being on the offensive. They tell outside spirits and other energetic intruders that they are not welcome.

Place the cap back on your ornament and hang it in the window closest to your back door. If you live in an apartment like I do, you can choose a window in an area where you feel the most spiritually vulnerable—for me that is my bedroom, for you that could be the living room or even the kitchen.

COMMUNICATING WITH YOUR ANCESTORS

Communication between you and your ancestors is a major part of connecting with them. By having conversations with spirits, you are signaling that you feel your relationship is valuable enough to give them your most precious resource: your time.

There are a few ways of communicating with your ancestors. I recommend trying a combination of them until you find one that suits both you and them.

Talking

Most of the time, simply speaking out loud to your ancestors can go a long way in building your relationship.

Admittedly, it can feel a little silly at first, but the more you do it, the more natural it will feel.

Take a few minutes each day to talk to your ancestors. Tell them stories and talk about things that are currently happening in your life.

When you begin to feel more comfortable with the process, you can even try asking them questions. And you may be surprised to learn that they have the ability to answer, if you're paying attention.

I find that answers appear in one of three ways.

The first is intuitively. Meaning you will just "know" the answer inside.

The second is by clairaudience, which is "hearing" the answer spoken to you.

The third is by way of signs and symbols you come across. For instance, if you ask an ancestor for their favorite flower and then all week you encounter lilies in various situations, you probably have received their answer.

Divination

The next method of communicating with your ancestors is through the practice of divination. Divination is the art of interpreting symbols in order to receive messages. Divination is typically performed with an instrument or object of some sort, such as a deck of tarot cards.

If you are a beginner, I recommend starting with either tarot reading or tea-leaf reading.

These two divination systems are chock-full of symbolism that your ancestors can use to communicate with you.

Divination can be the clearest and easiest way for you to communicate with both your ancestors and other spirits, because you both have something physical to focus on.

Dreams

Dreams are generally the first way our ancestors reach out to us.

Dreams are a glimpse into our subconscious minds. Dream symbolism is studied by witchcraft practitioners and psychologists alike, due to the wide range of symbols that appear to us in dreams.

I believe that when we are asleep, our spirits and the spirits of the dead can meet in a sort of neutral zone or spiritual plane and communicate with one another.

When we dream of our ancestors, these dreams tend to feel different than our regular ones. It is as though our senses get heightened. We can hear, see, and even touch our ancestors, as if they are there in the room.

Because these dreams can be very emotionally charged, messages can get muddled quickly upon waking. I recommend keeping a notebook and a pencil next to your bed so you can write down all the details quickly.

Remember: No symbol, word, or action is too small or insignificant to be recorded. You never know where a message may be revealed.

In all three of these communication styles, having an understanding of symbolism is imperative. Use the headstone symbols dictionary in chapter 9, "A Guide to Cemeteries," to get started with the fascinating language of the dead.

SPELL CASTING

While a lot of devotional work and self-improvement goes into an ancestor practice, it isn't without its benefits.

Your ancestors want good things for you and are willing to help you get them, and this is where spell casting comes into play.

Casting a spell is essentially just directing your energy, or the energy of other sources, in order to help you accomplish a goal.

Spells are essentially intent + energy = goal accomplishment.

Example

Let's say you want to build muscle and get stronger physically.

So, you make a plan. Each day you'll do ten to fifteen push-ups.

Your plan is your intent, the act of doing the push-ups is directing your energy, and by combining those, you get stronger and reach your goal.

Now, you can stick with just push-ups and you'll be successful, or you can bring in energy from other sources to help you get there faster.

In order to do that, you might bring in a personal trainer.

Now you have your intent and your energy, plus the energy and the expertise of your trainer, to help you get stronger faster or get stronger than you could just on your own.

Think of your ancestors as your trainers or personal support team. When you cast a spell, you can ask them to help it succeed or even to modify it to better serve you in the long term.

ACTIVITY: CRAFT A SPELL

I have created a spell template for you to use that can be altered to fit pretty much any circumstance you come across.

You can use the "Correspondences" section in the back of the book to tweak the ingredients to your liking.

What you need

An ancestor altar

Candle and candleholder

Dried herbs and flowers

Paper or parchment

Pen or pencil

Matches or a lighter

A fireproof dish

Astrological correspondences—for appropriate times to perform the spell

Optional: ritual ink or ancestor sigil—see chapter 2

Optional: additional offerings—see chapter 4

Instructions

First, you must think of your goal. This can be anything. Maybe you want to feel more confident or perhaps bring more financial prosperity into your life. A good rule of thumb with spellwork is to think about what is most needed in your life, not necessarily what is most wanted.

Next, you need to arrange all your ingredients and supplies on your ancestor altar.

This means that the candle is placed in a holder, the dried herbs and flowers are sprinkled around the candle or are placed on a dish nearby, and any other offerings you've chosen are arranged neatly.

When you feel ready, invite your ancestors to join you.

Write down your goal and light your candle.

Next, read your goal out loud and ask your ancestors if they can help you do what it takes to accomplish your goal.

Then carefully burn the paper in your fireproof dish and allow the candle to burn all the way through.

Thank your ancestors and either dispose of the herbs and flowers, any candle wax, and the ashes of the paper, or put them all in an envelope and keep it somewhere safe until your goal has been reached.

INCLUDING ANCESTORS IN DAILY LIFE

As you remember from the contract, or list of offerings, I made to my ancestors earlier in this chapter, I promised that I would include them in various activities in my day-to-day life.

When inviting your ancestors to join you in an activity, I recommend doing so on a case-by-case basis. Make sure your boundaries stay intact.

I find the following activities are really great for building a stronger relationship with ancestors.

Cooking or baking

Unless your ancestors were rich, and let's be real, for most of us that is not the case, it was probably up to them to grow and produce their own food. The first restaurant wasn't even created until the eighteenth century, in France, and unless your ancestors lived in an urban center, they likely didn't have access to specialized stores, such as bakeries or butcher shops.

Any one of your ancestors will be handy to call upon while cooking, but those who worked as farmers will be the best choice to help you craft nourishing and delicious meals.

Candlemaking

For millennia, fire was our only source of light in periods of darkness. Candles in particular have accompanied us through the last five thousand years. Candles have been there for us in moments of joy and celebration, like during the birth of a baby, as well as through periods of fear and sadness, like when a loved one takes their last breath.

Burning candles is a major component of both witchcraft and spirit work, so it can be enjoyable for your ancestors to participate in the process of making them with you.

Candles act as a guide for the spirits navigating both our world and theirs.

Reading and games

Activities such as reading and playing games allow you and your ancestors to have a little fun together.

One of my favorite pastimes in spirit work is to read out loud to my ancestors at the cemetery. I try to read a broad range of material to them, but works from their era always seem to go over well.

> Tip: While reading, give bibliomancy (divination by book) a try! Close your eyes, flip to a random page, and run your finger along it until you feel compelled to stop. Whatever word or line you land on could contain a message from your ancestors.

Another way to have fun and entertain your ancestors is by including them in games. Next time you find yourself playing Scrabble or cards with friends, silently ask a few ancestors to join you. Don't be surprised if you start receiving all the best tiles and cards.

> Tip: Make note of words, numbers, and even colors that appear in your games. There could be a message waiting for you.

Living well

Arguably the best way you can both include and honor your ancestors in your family life is by what I call living well.

Living well means you do what you can to make the most of your circumstances—to better your life, the lives of your descendants, and the lives of the people who live in your community.

Now, I don't mean that by living well people who face serious societal problems such as systemic racism or sexism can just wave a magic wand and make those issues disappear. It takes all of us to tackle those problems together.

What I do mean is that we can take the privileges and rights we do have and help make the world more equitable and better for us all.

Living well means different things to different people, but I have included three suggestions I have found to be very effective in my ancestor practice.

Learn personal finance

The divide between the rich and the poor has never been greater. During the COVID-19 pandemic, as many people struggled to pay rent and bills, large companies that control the majority of the world's wealth brought in record profits.

One of the most empowering things people can do is to learn personal finance. This is especially important for BIPOC and woman-identified people, as opportunities for growth are often deliberately squashed by the ruling class.

Financial literacy is the first step to building generational wealth, and it is our responsibility to become our own financial advocates from here on out.

Until 1974 in the USA, banks were legally allowed to refuse a single woman the ability to open a credit card in her name, and it wasn't much better for married women. While a married woman was allowed to set up a credit card, her husband was required to sign off.

My paternal grandparents didn't have a lot of money. They both worked way too hard while earning too little in order to provide the necessities for my dad and his brother. To compound the problem, there were periods in my grandfather's life when he struggled with gambling addiction, likely the result of his own trauma from growing up poor.

Because of this, they often faced difficult and uncertain times when it came to money. To make sure the kids had what they needed, my grandmother began hiding little bits of money when and where she could.

I know that one of her dreams for me would be to remain financially secure and independent, much like your ancestors would want for you.

While I am by no means perfect at personal finance, and I have struggled immensely, I have also done my best to learn what I can and apply those lessons to my life.

MY ADVICE FOR YOU

Read as many books on finance as you can and take a personal finance course. Be sure to check your local library for free resources.

Insist on being involved in all financial planning, budgeting, and investing—especially if you are married.

Talk openly about money with your kids (but please, never share stressful money news with them). Make sure you teach them the basics about saving and budgeting. Money is taboo in so many households; I didn't grow up learning to do anything related to banking. In fact, when I got my first paycheck at sixteen, I had to ask a stranger how to deposit it into the ATM.

But that small step of asking someone for help was a way for me to disrupt a negative pattern surrounding money passed down through my family line.

And finally, open a savings account and nickname it in honor of one of your ancestors. Every time you look at that account, you will think of them and remain motivated to save more.

Vote

Around the world, people have given their lives so that their community members may have the right to vote and to live in a democracy. You owe it not only to your own ancestors to exercise this right, but also to all the spirits who died to give it to you.

The road to voting rights has been paved with hardship. Countries that boast long democratic histories, such as Canada, have participated in the deliberate suppression of voting based on race and gender. In fact, First Nations and Inuit people were not granted the full right to vote until the 1960s! They faced not only genocide and the forceful seizure of their land, but also exclusion from any say in what happened to their home.

Voter oppression tactics have come back in full force as of late, so it is more important than ever to exercise our right to vote.

MY ADVICE FOR YOU

For the next five years, make a commitment to yourself and your ancestors that you will vote in every single election that you qualify for at every single level of government. Treat each race as if your vote is the deciding factor.

Research your candidates and know where they stand on issues you feel strongly about. When I vote, I look for candidates who are the most aligned with the future I envision for our world.

Volunteer for a political party or become a poll worker. You can help increase voter turnout and encourage people to do their civic duty.

Volunteer to drive people to and from the polls. Not everyone can get a full day off to vote or find a means of transportation. If you have the ability to help increase voter accessibility, you can be an active part of the solution.

Learn a language

Families who emigrate from non-English-speaking countries to English-speaking countries often face societal pressure to anglicize their identities and cut ties with their roots in order to avoid racist and prejudicial beliefs.

By learning a language—particularly one spoken by your ancestors—you are taking back the cultural heritage your family was forced to trade for safety.

Plus, on the side of the living, if you are able to communicate with a wider range of people, you will help make your community a more welcoming place for everyone.

I often think about how difficult it must have been for some of my ancestors who moved to Canada in the 1920s and '30s, knowing very little English and hoping things would work out all right in a new place.

I have begun learning the basics of Slovakian, Hungarian, and Greek in order to help me during my ancestral communication exercises.

MY ADVICE FOR YOU

Learn at least the basic greetings in one (or all) of your ancestral languages.

Request that your local library expand their language resource sections, and donate books in various languages if you can.

Advocate for government services and banks to expand the languages they offer to new residents of your country so that everyone has access to the resources they need.

If you already know multiple languages, volunteer your time to teach someone else or volunteer as a translator for new residents.

ANCESTRAL TRAUMA

Trigger warning: This section deals with topics that may be distressing, such as sexual assault.

Most of us who engage in ancestor work have some sort of trauma that impacts our daily lives, whether we are cognizant of it or not.

Trauma is the response our bodies and brains have to an upsetting event.

Some traumas affect entire nations and cultural communities, through situations such as colonialism, genocide, slavery, and war. Other traumas are individual or affect smaller family units, such as poverty, emotional abuse, and addiction. Sometimes these community traumas are the root cause of these individual traumas, but not always.

Trauma is the most unfortunate and unfair part of being a human, and can be categorized into four main groups.

Acute: Acute trauma is often the result of a single distressing event.

Chronic: Chronic trauma is the result of continuous or repeated distressing events.

Complex: Complex trauma is the result of multiple types of distressing events. Inherited or intergenerational trauma is often included in "complex" trauma.

Secondary: Secondary trauma is the result of hearing or seeing a distressing event that happens to another person.

The type of trauma looked at in ancestor work can be a combination of all of these, but the main focus is what is known as inherited trauma. Ancestor practitioners have long believed that trauma is handed down from one generation to the next on a spiritual level.

Spiritual people are not the only ones who believe this. In recent years, doctors and scientists have begun confirming that certain traumas may alter the way genes work, and that such traumas can be passed down from one generation to the next.

Essentially what this means is, they believe that when a distressing event happens to one person or group of people, it changes the way their offspring's genetics respond.

One study, known as the Dutch Hunger Study, has shown that offspring of people who were pregnant during the Dutch famine in World War II showed higher rates of obesity and diabetes throughout their lives. It is thought that their bodies had this response to experiencing a famine while in utero.

Spiritual bypassing and trauma

There is a persistent belief in the witchcraft community that when someone goes to the other side, everything becomes perfect and harmonious and all is forgiven...but I call bullsh*t.

Yes, I believe that our ancestors, in their new state of being, are provided with clarity and perspective on their lives. But that doesn't erase trauma, remove memories of injustice, or give a pass to those who inflicted pain on other people.

That sort of thinking is the epitome of spiritual bypassing.

Spiritual bypassing is the act of dismissing, downplaying, or ignoring our traumas and behaviors (or someone else's traumas and behaviors) and using spirituality and spiritual practices to do it.

Your ancestors are rooting for you and want you to succeed, but to say that they may not have residual anger, pain, concern, or sadness about what happened to them, and what they see happening to you, is unfair. There are things that cannot and should not be swept under the rug.

The belief that everything is hunky-dory when a spirit crosses over not only causes spiritual bypassing, but can also lead to suicidal ideation, which is a person's dangerous belief that everything will be fine if they end their life. As someone who was directly impacted by a loved one who died this way, I promise you it is not the answer.

Help is available.

Talk Suicide Canada: dial 833-456-4566
USA Suicide and Crisis Lifeline: dial 988

Note: Being justifiably upset about injustices and abuse doesn't automatically mean that someone is suffering on the other side. Each spirit deals with their trauma in their own way—just like the living.

My trauma

In order to help you understand trauma in a spiritual sense, I have decided to share part of my story and the traumas I work on.

Growing up, I was shy, and I was weird.

The type of kid whose sensitivity made them a prime target for bullies.

School was a constant battle for me. I tried various tactics to fit in over the years, such as befriending my bully (which never kept her from abusing me for long), as well as sometimes participating in the bullying of others in order to take the attention off myself—a decision that I wish I could undo.

These were survival mechanisms, and survival is a tricky thing, especially when you're a child. The child isn't logical; they're desperate and do what they need to in the moment.

I was bullied all day long, only to return home to an environment that was also chaotic and stressful. Home was filled with anger and sadness. I had no escape and nowhere felt safe, except when I was in the presence of my grandmothers.

My maternal grandmother, my baba, who is now in her eighties, provided me with much-needed structure and routine. She was also very encouraging of mental and creative pursuits, such as writing and drawing, an escape for a sensitive kid like me.

My paternal grandmother, my nana, who died when I was ten, provided me with much-needed affection and tenderness. She encouraged my sensitivity and gave me positive attention that I desperately craved.

Both provided me with the care and love I needed, though in different ways, but eventually I would return home or to school, where my torture resumed.

When I reached high school, things took a turn for the worse. The bullying reached an all-time high and now involved physical abuse as well as emotional.

Then, to make matters worse, a few months into grade nine, so around when I was fourteen turning fifteen, I was sexually assaulted in my *second* emotionally and physically abusive relationship, all while still trying to maintain a friendship with my childhood tormentor.

The days were absolutely unbearable. No amount of writing stories or kind, affirming words was going to help me. I rarely went to school at this point. In fact, as I write this, I still don't have my high school diploma or GED.

And then one day I found my holy grail, my savior: alcohol.

Alcohol couldn't stop what was happening to me externally, but it had this magical power of making me not care so much, while simultaneously encouraging me to be socially outgoing, engaging, and witty.

Alcohol was my best friend, my secret weapon.

Now, that relationship is dangerous and problematic in itself, but coupled with my genetics, it was a perfect storm.

You see, my paternal lineage is rife with addiction and alcohol abuse.

My dad's dad—my granddad—spent his entire life trying to maintain sobriety in the face of both alcohol and gambling addiction. His family was very poor, and his trauma surrounding that manifested in unhealthy coping mechanisms, just like it did for me.

My granddad's struggles and addiction brought chaos to the home, and that chaos was handed to my dad, which was then handed to me.

But there is a silver lining: each of us has done our best to end the cycle of using alcohol to cope. My granddad couldn't maintain his sobriety completely, but he tried. He may have passed the addiction cycle to us, but he also passed to us the cycle of trying to stop. And like before, this stopping idea was passed to my dad, and then to me, as well as other members of our family who live sober lifestyles.

What I want you to take away from this story is that the things that happened to you as a child and even a teenager are not your fault, and that you can work on bringing a new cycle of happiness and peace into the world for your descendants.

However, as much as I believe I am part of the healing journey for my ancestors, it is not something I can do on my own. It will take many people and generations to recover, and the same goes for your ancestral trauma. This isn't meant to discourage you from participating in the work, but rather to free you from the pressure to fix everything by yourself.

When I began the process of typing up this chapter, I heard a message clear as day from one of my ancestors. They said: "Tackling trauma is like being on the edge of a waterfall with only a paddleboat."

I take this to mean that you can't do it alone and you need resources to help you on your way. This is your trauma support team.

Your trauma support team

If part of your journey with your ancestors involves trauma, you need to assemble a support system—*preferably* before you begin. Remember, this is not something you can, or should, do on your own.

Therapist, psychiatrist, or other mental health professional

I believe that under no circumstances should anyone begin trauma work or crisis exploration without the support of a mental health professional. This process can be extremely taxing, and having someone trained to guide you is essential.

Remember: Therapy is not a punishment. Therapy is a beautiful gift you can give to yourself and your ancestors.

Living support

We all need friends and confidants in our corner who wish for us to be happy and healthy. When I think of this type of support, I think of my two grandmothers. Looking back, I see how their involvement helped shape me and provided me with certain skills that aid in this journey. Whom in your life can you count on to listen to or spend time with you?

Ancestor support

When I do any sort of trauma work, there are very specific ancestors I call upon for support. I know some of their names; some I don't know. Each member of this team has been affected by alcohol in one way or another. Some were the abusers of it themselves, while others were the spouses or children of those who struggled with addiction.

If you aren't sure whom exactly to call upon, you can try two different exercises.

EXERCISE 1: CALLING THE ANCESTORS

Take a look at your family or community tree (chapter 5) and randomly choose a few ancestors.

Ask them if they have the skills or capability to help you with your issue or situation.

Next, write down each of their names on a piece of paper, and assign them a sign or signal to give you if they say yes.

You want your sign to be specific enough that you know it's a message, and common enough that you will actually come across it, but not so common that it's a coincidence.

As an example, a few years ago I wanted to learn a second language as a hobby. I couldn't decide between Spanish and French, so I assigned them both a sign. Whichever I saw first would be the language I picked.

I assigned Spanish the image of a tiger, and French the image of a lion.

Immediately after deciding on this plan, I opened Instagram and the second image on my feed was one of a tiger.

If after a few days have passed, you haven't seen any of your signs, you can either try again by assigning new signals, or you can move on to exercise 2.

EXERCISE 2: THE ARCHETYPES

If you aren't sure where to start, the archetype ancestors (chapter 1) can be very helpful.

First, think about the qualities that surround your trauma. If it is something where you need strength, the protector archetype could be of use. Alternatively, if your trauma centers around communicating your needs, you may wish to turn to the teacher archetype.

Once you have decided which archetype may be best suited for the job, you can ask all of the ancestors who fall into that group to come forward and help you, if they are capable and have the skills to do so.

Remember to give them (and yourself) time to work on the issue together before switching archetypes.

ADVICE FOR BIPOC PRACTITIONERS

While I can provide many ancestor rituals and genealogy tips that apply to everyone regardless of culture or identity, there are some things that I don't have the authority to comment or advise on, such as the social and cultural impact and importance of ancestor work for BIPOC practitioners—especially WOC.

I felt it was essential to include some support and guidance directly from BIPOC practitioners who do have insight into some of the hopes, fears, benefits, and importance of this work within BIPOC communities.

Majorie Gatson

Majorie Gatson is a tarot reader, astrologist, and Reiki practitioner from Detroit who runs her business under the name the Punk Priestess. She predominantly uses divination in order to communicate with her ancestors and has learned in her work that different people require different tools or approaches. She also provides gentle encouragement for anyone nervous about starting ancestor work.

Majorie says

When connecting with ancestors from the other side, it is important to have inclusive tools to aid in your communication, especially if you are mixed race. I am also highly clairsentient, so I can sense when my loved ones are around me, and I can call on them when needed. By developing your clairvoyant abilities, you can connect better with your ancestors.

As a biracial American woman of color, I use multiple witchy practices when communicating with my ancestors. For my European ancestors, I find it easier to work with a pendulum and spirit board. They relate their messages to me by navigating my rose quartz crystal pendulum toward specific letters, zodiac signs, or numbers. They also communicate by swinging the pendulum in a yes or no direction when asked precise questions. I even use my tarot cards for them to select with my pendulum, so they have the option to facilitate messages this way as well. Many of my conversations with spirits have been very accurate when using the pendulum. Not only have their messages been confirmed by living relatives who knew them, but they are also able to provide me with direction on my life. The pendulum method, however, does not always work for some of my Black ancestors who were once enslaved. Many of my Black ancestors did not have the opportunity to be literate. When this is the case, I prefer to scry with crystals, where they can offer me guidance through images.

Being able to have a consistent and supportive connection with your loved ones from the other side can give your life more meaning, and it can make you feel safe in this unpredictable world. If you feel called to explore your guides, by all means honor that curiosity. I believe our ancestors are around us all the time and want to connect with us. Allow yourself to build that relationship, it will bring immense joy and love to your life.

Codi Popovich

Codi Popovich is a witch, tarot reader, metalsmith, and animal sanctuary owner living in Colorado and is known as Tarot Readings from a Bitch and Witch of Brush Hollow. Codi shares her anxieties about ancestor work and how she has eased into the practice by building connections through community and archetype ancestors.

Codi says

Ancestor work is something that I've always been nervous to approach. Coming from bloodlines of both colonizers and the colonized, I felt like it was a mess I should probably stay out of. Would my Indigenous ancestors want to speak to me? Do they harbor ill feelings toward me, as I am also part of those who snatched their children from the edges of the reservation? Do I even want to connect with the others? Matters, for me personally, are even more complicated because I have other ancestors who changed their names for their own safety while fleeing dangerous situations. I kept coming up against locked doors I wasn't sure I should even be knocking on. Discovering that I can also work with ancestors of community and archetypes has made me feel like I can give some ancestor work a shot, and maybe, eventually, pluck up the courage to try and connect with some ancestors of blood.

Adalinh Franck

Adalinh Franck is a folk witch, medium, tarot reader, and photographer from France who goes by the name the Hermit Witch Mama.

Adalinh shares the importance of ancestor worship in her Vietnamese culture and how she keeps this practice alive by way of altars, offerings, and honoring the legacy of her ancestors with her daughter.

Adalinh says

My family comes from different cultures, but my origins are mainly in Vietnam, where we practice what is called ancestor worship. It is an extremely old tradition, and it is customary for the eldest man of the family to take charge of it.

One essential part of this practice consists of erecting an altar for the dead, the Buddha, and the genies of the hearth in the most important room of the house.

Things such as photographs of the deceased, three different incense bowls, and two candles—which represent the moon and the sun—are commonly placed there. This altar is maintained religiously, and it is where we place our offerings; this acts as the area where we conduct our prayers. By tending this altar, we maintain a strong bond with our ancestors and in turn benefit from their protection and receive their blessings.

My practice consists of lighting a white candle every day for my deceased ancestors, as well as my spirit guides. I use white because it symbolizes mourning in Asia. I also burn traditional incense for them, as well as a special paper called Hell notes. Hell notes are a currency that the spirits use in the afterlife to pay for things and conduct business.

During each holiday and especially on Têt (Vietnamese New Year), I invite my ancestors to join us in our home and share in these important moments and celebrations. For these occasions, I like to serve them the dishes they taught me to make, as well as give them gifts of the things they loved during their lifetime. All of these offerings are placed against the top of my forehead before I offer them. This is a customary practice that represents protection.

My spiritual and occult practices are a way of honoring my ancestors that were engaged in witchcraft, divination, and shamanism. I also perpetuate certain precepts that they instilled in me and work not to reproduce behaviors and systems of thought in conflict with my personal values.

My worship also allows me to practice forgiveness and healing. Through this, I hope to help them ascend as spirits and heal my family lineage. I try to honor their journey, their sacrifices, as well as thank them for everything they've done. Finally,

I make a point of regularly talking about them with my daughter so their stories can be told for a long time to come and not be forgotten.

CHAPTER FOUR

ANCESTOR ALTAR AND OFFERINGS

Ancestor Altar and Offerings

WHAT IS AN ALTAR?

An altar is a designated structure for the purpose of establishing a spiritual connection with a spirit or deity—a place to make offerings in their honor or to perform other rituals.

Altars are central to the human experience and play an important role in our lives. To wit, the "big events," such as weddings, funerals, and other religious ceremonies, usually take place at an altar of some sort.

Whether a person lived two thousand years ago or just two years ago, chances are they had an interaction with an altar or other sacred space at some point in their lifetime.

Altars are not specific to one group of people or religion. No matter where your ancestors hail from, they have some sort of history with an altar. Rituals and rules may vary, but altars all serve a common purpose: worship.

Altars come in a wide range of types, styles, and sizes.

In the Vatican, for example, one of the main altars people go to visit is underneath St. Peter's Baldachin, an elaborate baroque-style canopy sculpted in bronze. In contrast, the ancient Druids in Ireland used large stone slabs known as cromlechs for their altars. Neither is more special than the other. They're just different.

ANCIENT ALTARS

Ancient China

Because China has the longest continuous history in the world, it is home to thousands of altars. Some are ancient, some are modern, and some are still waiting to be discovered.

In 1993, in a remote area of the Xinjiang Uyghur Autonomous Region, a 328-foot-long sun altar was found that dates back to the Bronze Age three thousand years ago!

Altars of this particular design had been found in more southeastern parts of China already, so this discovery confirmed the existence of a strong link between the different cultures who lived in this massive country.

Ancient Egypt

Of course, one cannot talk about altars without mentioning the ancient Egyptians, who had complex and beautiful religious systems that included various altars within their spiritual practices.

The Egyptians situated elaborate altars in the grand temples and pyramids, as well as keeping smaller ones in houses or gardens that served as places for daily worship.

Like all altars, their function was to provide a place to meet with their gods and to leave an offering for them. Though the Egyptians did ask for favors, the main purpose seemed to be to honor the deities and show appreciation for them, in hopes of affording the people a brighter future. If you care for your gods, they will care for you.

Ancient Rome

The ancient Romans kept many altars—from long-established structures to random rocks and stones cobbled together at a moment's notice.

The Romans were extremely pious and did not make decisions without consulting the various gods and oracles. And where did the gods like to hang out? Altars made in their honor, of course.

In ancient Rome, altars were used as places of worship, places of refuge, and places of sacrifice. Due to the Roman influence around Europe, many Roman ideas surrounding altars are still ingrained in modern paganism, as well as Christianity.

The ara pacis, or altar of peace, was an altar used by the Romans for animal sacrifices, which were common in ancient Rome as rituals invoking the gods' protection or help with various community issues.

The Romans also considered their own homes to be places of worship.

Every household had their own altar set up where they could ask the gods and goddesses for help with everyday matters, as well as pay tribute to them in the form of offerings.

Worship took place twice a day, in the morning and the evening, and could be performed with other members of the family or in private.

All public Roman altars were places of refuge. They were meant to provide spiritual and physical asylum, a place where one could seek out the protection not only of deities but also of the elders and community leaders who spent time there.

This idea of the church being a place of refuge is still seen today in Roman Catholicism; the Church has a duty to protect those in need. Churches are meant to be a safe haven for everyone regardless of personal circumstances.

ANCESTOR ALTARS

What is an ancestor altar?

An ancestor altar is a set place where you can connect with the spirits of your ancestors, both recent and ancient.

Do I need one?

While I consider most things in a spiritual practice to be optional, the ancestor altar is not one of those things. That's not to say it has to look a specific way or contain

specific items. It should be a place where you feel comfortable and that accurately represents who you and your family are in terms of style. All of the decorative and spiritual suggestions for your altar in this chapter are just that: suggestions.

An ancestor altar is a place for you to honor your ancestors, a place to grieve your ancestors, and a place to communicate with your ancestors.

Altars are a focal point for you, and an anchor for the spirits

"Anchor" is a term you will come across a lot in this book. A **spiritual anchor** is something such as an object (or sometimes a place) that draws the spirit of a deceased person in. Usually these are objects that the spirit has a connection to, either literally or symbolically.

When the spirit of a person can find something with their energy attached to it, it makes it easier for them to come into the physical plane; and when you have something you can focus on in order to call them, building a connection becomes much easier.

But aren't I already connected to my ancestors by virtue of being related to them?

Of course you are! But that doesn't mean you can't make that connection stronger, and if you can, why wouldn't you? Some ancestors will come through easily, but others will require more effort, especially if you have never met them.

An ancestor altar also provides you with a reason for consistency, which in my opinion is the most important part of any spiritual practice. In this age of social media, there has been a rise in what is known as lazy witchcraft. The lazy witch expects everything to be handed to her, without putting in any work herself. It's important to remember that nobody can build your ancestor practice but you, and the easiest way to get started is by crafting an altar.

PLANNING YOUR ALTAR

Before you begin the physical process of creating the altar, you will need to consider how many altars you want for the different types of ancestors in this book.

I will briefly cover different altar types in this section, but the main altar you will learn to make is the one for your blood ancestors.

For some of you, making one big altar for blood ancestors, community ancestors, and the archetypes will work fine, while others prefer to give each their own space.

Things to consider

Space, privacy, and time.

If you live in a small studio apartment, you probably don't have the space for multiple altars.

If you have roommates, they may not want to see your altars in and around communal living spaces.

If you have a hectic schedule, finding the time to give each altar enough attention may be difficult.

DESIGNING YOUR ANCESTOR ALTAR

The most important thing to decide when designing your ancestor altar is whether you want all of your blood ancestors to be together or not. While I currently have both my maternal and my paternal ancestors on the same altar, for a long time I worked with just my paternal ancestors.

Each family is unique.

Just because you have DNA from both maternal and paternal lines, that doesn't mean you need to include them in your altar space (or in your practice).

You can have as few or as many altars as you see fit.

The altar furniture

Deciding what furniture to use for your altar comes down to personal preference and what is accessible to you.

Heirloom furniture: Heirlooms are covered in more depth in chapter 7, but you may want to consider using an inherited piece for your altar.

Existing furniture: You don't need to run out and buy a bunch of new things for your altar. The top of a nightstand or bookshelf can work perfectly.

Storage: Small shelves like spice racks and other petite storage compartments are a wonderful addition to your altar for housing things like graveyard dirt, decorations, and offerings.

Note: If you practice a specific spiritual tradition that has its own rules about ancestor veneration and ancestor altars, I recommend following those guidelines.

DECORATIONS AND OFFERINGS

What is the difference between a decoration and an offering?

Decorations are permanent (or long-term) items on your altar that act as continuous anchor points for a spirit.

Popular decorations for ancestor altars are things like photographs, heirlooms and keepsakes (chapter 7), figurines, maps, flags, plants, cremains, and graveyard dirt.

I will be teaching you how I collect graveyard dirt later in this chapter, as well as going over some of the objects I have on my altar.

The beauty of decorations is that they are completely unique to you and your family, and you can make your altar look however you'd like it to.

Offerings are temporary. They are something you gift to your ancestors. Though they may only last from a few moments to a few days, the emotional and spiritual effects of offerings are enduring and help establish a relationship between you and your ancestors.

Offerings fall into three categories: time, words, and things.

Time as an offering is the practice of showing up for your ancestors. Setting aside a portion of your day to perform a ritual or work with your ancestors is the most important offering you can give. It shows that you are dedicated to them.

Words as an offering are the process of speaking to your ancestors. Divination and other forms of spirit communication fall into this category. Getting to know your ancestors' needs and boundaries, as well as sharing your own, will be beneficial to your relationship.

Things are the physical items you give to your ancestors. Think water, coffee, food, trinkets, flowers, and other such gifts.

Though they differ only slightly, both decorations and offerings are important components of your ancestor altar used to honor the spirits.

INSTRUCTIONS

The process of prepping your space and putting together your altar should be completed over three days: the day before the full moon, the day of the full moon, and the day following the full moon. This is because we can use the moon's energy to heighten any of the spiritual work we do.

Many calendars are available online that will tell you the correct dates and times to perform the ritual for your specific time zone.

The following instructions and rituals can be performed as many times as you feel is necessary.

Day before the full moon

The day before the full moon is the last part of the moon's waxing cycle.

The waxing period is when the illumination of the moon is increasing from 1 percent to 99 percent, and is all about building and growing something. Anything you do now will channel an abundance of spiritual strength.

Cleansing your space

The first step in building any type of altar is to properly cleanse and bless your space both physically and spiritually.

By cleansing on the waxing moon, you are signaling to your ancestors that qualities such as peace, contentment, structure, and protection are what you expect not only to receive from your ancestor relationship, but to provide to them as well.

Remember that your ancestors will be guests in your home. You wouldn't invite your living relatives to your place when it's piled high with dishes, dirt, and dust, so don't do it when inviting your dead family over, either.

Start by cleaning your home from top to bottom. Make sure you dust in all the little cracks and crevices. Take your time and be thorough.

Open your windows and allow the stale air to leave and fresh air to enter.

Next, you will want to wash your floors with your regular detergent and allow them to dry fully. This is to help get out the last of the dirt before you perform the spiritual portion of the cleansing.

After your floors are dry, you need to do a ritual washing of the space. The following recipe costs only a few dollars and is safe for homes with both cats and dogs.

Cleansing Floor Wash

What you need

Two or three chamomile tea bags—for calm and serenity

Two or three lemon balm tea bags—for memory and communication

A large bowl, a bucket, and a mop

Place your tea bags in a large bowl and pour boiling water over them.

While the tea bags steep, fill a bucket with warm water.

When your tea water is a pale golden shade, pour it into your bucket.

Now wash your floors, beginning at your front door and ending at your back door, or where your back door would be located if you don't have one. If you're so inclined, you can also wash both doors with the mixture.

> **Tip:** Tea can stain, so don't use this mixture on anything white. If this is a concern, replace the tea with a few drops of chamomile and lemon balm essential oils.

Once your washing is complete, it is time to add some protective energy. Protection should be added into your space in layers. Remember, the more layers you can create, the better.

Incense

Burning herbs and plants for ceremonial reasons is deeply embedded in many different cultures.

The best way to choose which plants to burn is to take your own culture into account. You can honor your ancestors in a way that is familiar to them while adding protection into the space with the smoke.

If you don't know much about which plants your ancestors used (or you don't feel comfortable performing a ritual because of potential appropriation), you can choose a type of incense based on your own personal taste.

A scent you like can instill a space with positivity, and positivity is the best type of protection there is.

Broom Protection Charm

This charm is designed to protect your home and infuse it with different positive energies.

Brooms are a staple in many witchcraft traditions and have long been associated with witches and cunning women.

They represent the sanctity of a space and offer protection to all those who cross the threshold of a home.

Brooms also have strong symbolic ties to fertility and prosperity, so keeping one above your door can encourage those energies, which is great for helping an ancestor practice grow and prosper.

What you need

A broom—preferably made of natural materials, such as broomcorn or wood. Craft and home decor shops often have small decorative ones that work beautifully for this purpose.

Ribbon—six-inch pieces of white, black, red, green, blue, purple, pink, yellow, and orange. These represent different energies (page 267).

Directions

Tie each ribbon around the handle of the broom and hang it on the back of your entry door inside your home.

Day of the full moon

On the day of the full moon, the moon's surface is 100 percent illuminated by the light of the sun. The full moon is the height of lunar power. It is when the energy is at its peak.

While the moon is technically only revealed at 100 percent for a few moments, the energy does linger for eight to twelve hours, so don't be discouraged if you can't start this next step at the exact right moment.

The full moon represents fertility, unlimited potential, and a new life. All of our ancestors have used the moon as a calendar and guide at one time or another, regardless of culture or region. This makes it the perfect energy to build your altar under.

Because you did your prep work the previous day, you can get started putting together the altar (or altars) as soon as the moon reaches its zenith, but if you'd like to light some incense or play some music, feel free.

This experience should be enjoyable but still have a certain amount of seriousness to it.

Begin by stating your intention out loud. Talking to your ancestors is an important part of this work. Go over why you are building the altar, what its purpose is (anchor), and what you hope to get out of beginning this journey with them.

You may also wish to record any feelings or thoughts that arise during this process on a blank page in your BOA (page 20).

Once you are happy with your altar setup, you are done for the day. It can be tempting to immediately start giving offerings, but it is important to let the energy settle a little bit before diving in.

Day after the full moon

The day after the full moon is when the illumination of the moon's surface begins to dwindle from 99 percent to 1 percent, a progression known as the waning cycle.

The waning cycle is about changes and endings, and death is the biggest change and ending there is. I like to refer to the waning cycle as the intuitive phase, the time each month when we retreat into our minds and our bodies.

It may seem counterintuitive to begin a practice during this phase, but you must remember that ancestor work is rooted in death.

The formal invitation

What you need

Your BOA

A candle and candleholder

Any offerings you would like to gift your ancestors

In chapter 3, "Working with Your Ancestors," I asked you to map out your boundaries and rules in regard to your ancestors and other spirits. Now it is time to put this into action.

Place your candle in the holder and light it. Place your other offerings on the altar and describe them to your ancestors—tell them what they are and whom they are meant for.

Next, you are going to read your boundaries out loud. Even though you spoke to your ancestors about the altar the previous day, as well as while you read the chapter "Working with Your Ancestors," this ritual is the formal invitation.

What you do next is up to you, but I do recommend letting the candle burn all the way through.

Letting the candle finish reinforces the idea that time is your most important offering. You want to start off on the right foot by not rushing.

ALTAR ANCHOR SUGGESTIONS

While the majority of your decorations will be heirlooms or other things of that nature, there are a few staples I believe every altar can benefit from.

Think of your ancestor altar as a little home for the spirits. Each anchor you place is like adding a new room or piece of furniture. You are outfitting a space where you and your antecedents can gather and commune.

Grave dirt

Before you begin collecting grave dirt, please read chapter 9, "A Guide to Cemeteries," in its entirety.

Grave dirt is one of the best spirit anchors there is. Your ancestor's grave or resting place is their body's home, and dirt from the grave gives them something easy to focus on. Grave dirt can be used for both your blood ancestors and your community ancestors. I recommend working with a community ancestor for a minimum of two years before you collect some of their dirt. Because you're not family, you must spend the time building the relationship.

While some people collect grave dirt (or graveyard dirt) for use in spells and other rituals, the grave vessels I am teaching you to make are meant to be kept permanently on your ancestor altar.

During your research, you will likely come across the locations of some of your ancestors' graves, but if for some reason you don't, there are alternatives that can be used in place of the dirt. These alternatives can also be a wonderful way to honor the ancient ancestors whose graves you may never find.

What you need

Small Ziploc bags

Labels

Glass jars that fit on your altar (I recommend 1- to 2-ounce jars)

Grave locations

A small spade or spoon

Appropriate offerings (time, words, or things—use this chapter in conjunction with chapter 9, "A Guide to Cemeteries," to help you choose)

Directions

> Tip: Pick a sunny and dry day! If it has rained recently, you may need to allow for more time during step 5.

Step 1: The process of collecting grave dirt begins even before you set foot in the cemetery. Take a few days to decide whose grave you want dirt from, start planning which offerings you will bring, and get your cemetery kit ready (pages 223–25).

Step 2: Next, take your small Ziploc bags and label each one with an ancestor's name and plot number. Each ancestor should have their own bag and their own jar.

Step 3: Head to the cemetery, using chapter 9 as your guide. If this is your first time visiting your ancestors, I don't recommend collecting dirt; instead, use this time to bond. However, if you are not local to the area it may be your only chance to collect. Do what feels right for you.

Step 4: Collect your dirt. Digging around graves can attract unwanted attention from the living, so you may wish to have some flowers or plants with you so it appears as though you are doing some regular headstone maintenance and aren't doing anything illegal or disrespectful. Plus, your flowers can double as an offering.

Cemeteries often have planting guides available online or in their office. Always follow the rules laid out by the cemetery. I cover tools and supplies you should bring to the cemetery on pages 223–25. If you are planning on collecting dirt, you should have a small spade to dig with. A spoon also works in a pinch.

As you are collecting your dirt, state your intention about why you are taking it and what you are giving in exchange (and never renege on this deal).

Some find it helpful to ask their ancestor's permission and wait a few moments for a response before they begin to collect. Though most of your ancestors will be fine with the arrangement, it doesn't automatically mean they all will be. Your response will likely come intuitively, and a no is generally pretty obvious, such as a gut feeling or an external sign.

Step 5: After your dirt is collected and you are back home, it's time to dry it out. This step takes around a week even for small amounts of soil. You want your grave dirt completely dried out before you bottle it, to avoid unwanted growth.

Either open the Ziploc bags and place them in a sunny spot near a window, or pour the contents of each into their own (labeled) bowl. Every few days, turn over the soil so everything has a chance to dry.

Step 6: Label each glass jar with the name or initials of your ancestor and transfer the dry dirt to its new home. If you'd like, you can mix in some dried flowers or herbs as an offering.

If you have leftover dirt, you can either return it, use it in spells, sprinkle it around your front door, or add it to potted plants around your home.

Step 7: Place the grave dirt securely on your altar. You may wish to light a candle or make an offering to help the energy of the earth you collected, as well as the attached spirits, settle in.

Alternatives to grave dirt

There are many reasons why you may not have access to the graves of your ancestors. They could be in a different country, or in an unknown location, or perhaps your ancestors were cremated.

Symbolic grave dirt

This plant-based alternative can be used as a substitute for grave dirt.

What you need

A jar and a label

Dried willow bark, cedar, juniper, and rose petals

A mortar and pestle

A charcoal disk (the hookah kind)

A fireproof container, such as a caldron

A bowl

Paper and a pen

Dirt or soil from your home or a favorite place

Directions

Step 1: First you need to decide who this symbolic grave dirt will honor. As you would if you were gathering actual grave dirt, you will want to arrange an offering or a deal of some sort. I find making a donation to a charitable organization in my ancestor's name works really well.

Label your jar with the name of the ancestor.

Step 2: Next, grind your plant material with the mortar and pestle. The goal isn't to create a fine powder but rather to just break the material up a bit. By manually combining it, you are putting some of your energy into the mixture.

Step 3: Light your charcoal disk and put it in the bottom of your fireproof dish or caldron. While it is getting nice and hot, take your paper and write your ancestor's name on it.

Step 4: When the charcoal is completely lit, start adding small bits of your plant mixture to the charcoal and letting it burn to ash. Little by little, add more and burn. When all of the mixture is burned, add the paper containing your ancestor's name and let it burn to ash as well.

Step 5: Let the charcoal and ash cool completely. Then pour the entire contents of the fireproof dish or caldron into a bowl. Add your dirt or soil and mix everything together.

Step 6: Bottle your symbolic grave dirt and place it on your ancestor altar.

Get creative

There are many additional options for creating or using symbolic dirt.

I have a great-great-great-grandfather who was killed in a mine collapse in Scotland. As far as I can tell, his body was never recovered. Since I can't collect dirt from his grave, I opted to fill a bottle with coal and rock fragments to represent his resting place.

If you have access to a property your ancestors lived on, collecting dirt from there can be a great option. Perhaps if they were big churchgoers, some dirt from the churchyard can be used as well. This is also a great option for community ancestors.

> **Warning:** If you do go the churchyard route, be aware of any graves located there; you don't want to accidentally bring home a stranger!

Another option could be to make grave dirt for one ancestor out of the dirt from your other ancestors' graves. If you have dirt from the graves of your father's parents but none from your father's grave, you can combine his parents' dirt in equal parts to represent him.

And of course, if you have the cremains of an ancestor, they should be housed on your ancestor altar as well.

Slate tile

A piece of slate is an inexpensive way to represent the hearth of your altar home. The hearth has long been thought of as the "heart" or center of the home. It is where people gathered to cook, keep warm, tell stories, and even perform magic and other rituals.

I like to think of slate as being symbolic of security, sustenance, and support. Wherever you keep a piece of slate, you are encouraging those energies.

Slate should be used for your blood ancestor altar and any areas where you need extra energy, such as in your kitchen or work space.

Slate tiles can be found at almost any craft or home improvement store.

Rocks

Rocks are another inexpensive way to enhance your altar. Rocks represent the earth and are a stable foundation for the altar home. Rocks are what everything else is built upon. They are the foundation of our planet.

By placing a rock or stone in a sacred space, you are bringing in calming and secure energy.

Rocks procured from ancestral lands can be a wonderful way to represent your ancient ancestors as well.

Rocks also helped create some of our first graves. Human remains have been found inside caves and at Stone Age structures such as Newgrange in Ireland, and from ancient times, simple rock piles known as cairns protected bodies from both animals and the elements. Not to mention that headstones have been cut and carved from rock for centuries.

Red thread charm

In witchcraft, the red thread represents the bloodline. This can be the literal bloodline, meaning your DNA and genetic relationships, or it can be a spiritual or symbolic bloodline, such as a shared quality or specific rank within a group of people.

The concept of the red thread appears in many different cultures. In Gaelic folk magic, it is used in a variety of spells and charms; in some Jewish and Slavic cultures, red thread bracelets are worn as a form of protection and for luck. And in Chinese mythology, the red thread represents fate and partnerships.

The red thread plays a major part in ancestor work, as it provides something symbolic that connects and binds us to one another.

Throughout this book you will discover several ways to incorporate red (and other color) threads, strings, and ribbons into your work.

This craft is a small protective charm to hang on your altar.

What you need

Three equal lengths of red thread: embroidery twine, wool, and simple cord all work well

Rose hydrosol (hydrosol is the water extracted when making essential oils)

RED THREAD

(2-oz. Hanks),

4/3

FANCY

SPACED

4/6

Per lb.

SMALL REEL.   MIDDLE SIZE REEL.

3/3 per gross.   **3/6** per gross.

…t known Brand in RED

RED THREAD

100 yards on a spool,

Crochet Yarn.

100 yards on a spool,

Price, **4/-** per dozen.

1 doz. spools in a box.

Put up in 1 doz. boxes, also in cases containing
1 gross assorted best shades.

No extra charge for case.

NET PRICES.

For this exercise, we use three red threads to represent the past, present, and future.

Roses come with an abundance of folklore and spiritual associations. Since they grow in almost every place on earth, they are one of the best all-purpose plants to incorporate into your practice. The Romans had a custom of placing a rose above the table during important political and social discussions; this meant that any conversations taking place within the room were to remain secret. This is where the term "sub rosa," or "under the rose," originates.

Directions

Step 1: First soak your red threads in the rose hydrosol for a few hours.

Step 2: Remove the threads and let them dry completely.

Step 3: Simply braid your three strands together and hang the braid next to or on your altar.

More suggestions

Flags: National flags are a thoughtful and inexpensive way to honor your ancestors. Flags of every nation can be found in almost any big-box or dollar store. You can also add community flags, such as LGBTQ2S banners, to honor those ancestors as well.

Flowers and plants: Go through the plants of the dead list on pages 227–31 and choose one to keep on your altar. The spirits of plants can help facilitate different things for your ancestor relationships, such as reconciliation, protection, peace, and even mourning. When the flowers have passed their prime, be sure to dry them out to use in spells.

Charms or figurines: These are great for honoring your community ancestors. On my altar I have a small howling wolf figurine to represent the part of my paternal lineage that comes from Bury St. Edmunds, as well as all the people from that part of Suffolk, England.

Skeletons and poppets: While technically these are figurines, skeletons and poppets (small human-shaped figures of clay, cloth, or even wood) can be used as spiritual vessels for your ancestors to occupy.

RECORD OF OFFERINGS

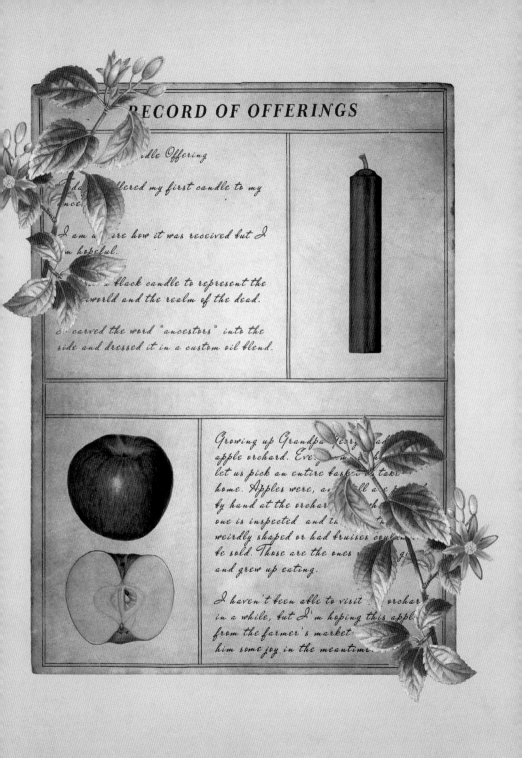

...dle Offering

I da...llered my first candle to my
ancei...

I am u...ire how it was received but I
...m hopeful.

...a Black candle to represent the
...world and the realm of the dead.

...carved the word "ancestors" into the
side and dressed it in a custom oil blend.

Growing up Grandpa Terry...ad...
apple orchard. Eve...
let us pick an entire bask...take
home. Apples were, a...ll a...p...
by hand at the orchar...h...
one is inspected and t...h...
weirdly shaped or had bruises coul...
be sold. Those are the ones...g...
and grew up eating.

I haven't been able to visit...orchar...
in a while, but I'm hoping this appl...
from the farmer's market...
him some joy in the meantim...

Mini-urns and mini-headstones: These are another great way to represent the ancestors whose grave locations remain a mystery. On pages 200–203 of the cemetery chapter, you will find a fun craft for making your own mini-headstones.

Specialized objects: Specialized objects are things that your ancestors would use on a daily basis. For example, if your great-grandfather was a physician, an antique stethoscope would make a great altar item. If you are a writer and want to honor your community ancestors who were also writers, copies of their works or even nice pens and pencils make great anchors.

CHAPTER FIVE

FAMILY TREE

Family Tree

WHAT IS A FAMILY TREE?

A family tree is a graphic map that charts your ancestry and lineage. Each branch of the tree depicts a different generation, connected by lines that represent the links between individuals, beginning with you.

Creating a family tree can be helpful for visualizing your ancestry, especially if that is the way you learn best.

I would like to preface this section by saying that your family tree can look however you want it to look. Historically, a family tree's main focus has been on parents and the various grandparents and great-grandparents you are genetically descended from. These trees have also typically followed a strict gender binary that isn't exactly in touch with our modern world.

Family trees can be triggering and upsetting if only "traditional family" arrangements are considered "correct."

While I use the terms "paternal" and "maternal" to describe my parents and the genetic lines they represent, those terms may not fit you or your family.

If the person who gave birth to you is a trans man, you may want to refer to his branch of the tree as the paternal line.

If you have two mothers, their branches may both be called maternal lines.

You could even just refer to each line by number—for example, branch one and branch two, or perhaps parent one and parent two.

Children of single parents or people who have distanced themselves from certain family lines may want to work with only one branch of ancestors, whereas adopted people may have multiple lines they want to include.

How your tree represents your family is totally up to you. Nobody can tell you which way is right and which way is wrong. There is no use making a tree if every time you look at it, it stirs up painful feelings—so let your tree reflect your beliefs.

> **If someone was abusive and you don't want them to appear in your tree, please know that you have every right to exclude them without guilt or shame.**

CREATING A FAMILY TREE: BLOOD ANCESTORS

As I mentioned in chapter 2, "Ancestor Grimoire," I have four separate ancestor grimoires for my blood ancestors.

This means that I have four different family trees that cover my blood ancestors. Of these four, two have many branches containing many names, while the other two are sparse and full of gaps, as they are works in progress.

Despite my having spent more time with some ancestors than with others, all of these trees and the people who occupy them are sacred to me. When I look at them, I think, "Here are my people, here are my ancestors."

Designing your family tree should be fun. This is where you should experiment and play around with different ideas, styles, and colors. I associate specific colors and flowers with my ancestors, so I opted to incorporate those in my design.

Perhaps you are drawn to the classic style where everyone gets their own leaf, or maybe a minimalist chart of neatly typed names is more your thing.

I recommend titling each family tree with your ritual ink (recipe on page 25) and marking the corner with your ancestor sigil (directions on pages 25–26).

Tip: Don't worry about how many ancestors you can identify right at the start. Just begin by filling in the names and relationships you know. In time, as you work on the research portion of your ancestry, you will uncover more and more people.

I have included a portion of my family tree on page 91 for you to look at if you are feeling stuck.

I recommend that you place your family tree at the beginning of your BOA for easy access.

From a practical standpoint, it can be helpful to be able to flip open your BOA to quickly confirm a relationship between two ancestors or double-check the spelling of a name. You may think you will remember everyone in your tree, but once you go back even a few generations, you may be dealing with hundreds of individuals, and it can get confusing fast. There is no shame in needing to refresh your memory.

When many of your ancestors are grouped together like this, there is strength in numbers. If you find yourself needing a mental or spiritual boost, you can turn to this page and ask for whoever is available to turn up and help out.

CREATING A FAMILY TREE: COMMUNITY ANCESTORS

When it comes to creating a community tree, a lot of people aren't sure where to begin. The biggest problem they encounter is that many of these spirits are not related to one another (or to us) in a close genetic way, so they aren't sure where they are supposed to place the lines.

It's important to remember that the connection you feel to these ancestors is spiritual. It is because you share the same energy in one or more facets of your identity that you have become related.

I recommend keeping your identity ancestors in separate trees based on which communities they belong to (even though they are all part of the broader community ancestors group). However, it's okay to repeat ancestors, as some of them may overlap and appear in multiple community trees.

Our blood ancestors can also be put into our community trees. For example, I am a sober person since giving up alcohol in 2018; therefore, I feel a kinship with the community of people who have been addicted to substances and given them up. It just so happens that a few of those people are also my genetic ancestors.

As with your blood ancestors chart, style, color, and design are totally up to you. One benefit of these charts is that you can really get creative with the layout.

Here's how I build my community family tree: I place my name in the middle and then arrange all of the ancestors in a circle around me. From there I use a line to connect each one to me.

If you want, you can go further and add qualities you admire or some impactful stories about each ancestor on the chart and connect those with lines as well. It's a nice little touch that lets the ancestors know what effect they have had on your life.

Place your community tree in the community ancestors section of your BOA. This page can be turned to when you need advice or support about major life decisions.

CREATING A FAMILY TREE: ARCHETYPE ANCESTORS

Creating this tree is a lot of fun because you have the opportunity to include a wide range of spirits.

Not only will your blood and community ancestors have a space on this chart, but so will important spiritual figures, such as deities, nonhuman spirits, and characters from folklore who embody the archetypes.

Start this tree by writing down each archetype on a different section of the page.

From there, you can begin adding ancestors to each group, connecting them to their archetype by a line. Remember, it is totally fine if some people appear in multiple spaces.

I personally don't include myself in this tree, as I do not know what archetype I will represent to my descendants. If you are in the same position, write a little request at the bottom of the page asking whoever inherits your BOA to place you somewhere.

In chapter 1, I assigned each archetype a candle color; incorporating these hues into your design can add a nice layer of energy.

Place your archetype tree in the archetype ancestors section of your BOA. This page can be turned to when you need to embody the qualities of these ancestors yourself or when you are looking to bring those energies into your home.

OTHER IDEAS FOR YOUR TREES

While I do strongly recommend keeping your trees in your BOA, there are some other ways they can be incorporated into your home or ancestor altar area.

The first option, of course, is to frame and display them. This lets visitors (of the living and the dead variety) know who is protecting you and your space.

Your family tree display doesn't need to be made of paper. Cross-stitching your tree onto fabric or woodburning it into a board is a creative and energetically charged way to honor your relatives.

Having your trees out in the open can act as an anchor that attracts other ancestors you may not know yet. For these spirits, seeing the names of their parents or cousins or great-great-great-grandchildren can work as an invitation to join the group and reach out to you. This is because there is power in a name.

As with all things related to spirit and ancestor work, don't forget to assert your boundaries if need be.

NAMING TRADITIONS

Once you have filled in areas of your family trees, you may notice that patterns emerge in the names.

Names are an important symbol. They tell the world who someone is.

Sometimes names are meant to describe characteristics, such as Mabel, which means "lovely," or Kwan, which means "strong."

Other times they simply say, "This is the son of Thomas," as does the surname Thompson.

Our names are chosen for us, and we wear them every day. For some, this is affirming; for others they don't quite fit.

Many cultures have naming traditions, and understanding them can help you connect with your ancestors. Below are a few of my favorites.

Nigerian naming tradition

One of the traditions that best shows the impact of community in naming comes from the Yoruba people in southwest Nigeria.

Seven days after a baby is born (so the eighth day of life), family elders gather and decide on a name for them. The name typically tells a story about the circumstances of the birth. There are names for when a baby arrives by breech delivery, and for the time of day they joined the world—basically any scenario you can think of has an associated name. And if for some reason there isn't one, all the elders will put in their suggestions and each option will be discussed.

Like all traditions, this one has variations. For some families, the name represents hopes and dreams they have for the child, rather than the circumstances of their birth.

English naming tradition

Though not followed as closely today as in earlier times, the English naming tradition was created to honor those who came before.

There can be slight variations in the system, but generally the pattern goes like this:

- The first son is named after the father's father.
- The first daughter is named after the mother's mother.
- The second son is named after the mother's father.
- The second daughter is named after the father's mother.
- The third son is named after the father.
- The third daughter is named after the mother.
- The fourth son is named after the father's eldest brother.
- The fourth daughter is named after the mother's eldest sister.

After that, the pattern can continue through siblings or be abandoned altogether.

Scottish naming traditions are similar in terms of first names; however, when it comes to surnames, women have the option of keeping their maiden name, taking their spouse's name, or using them both.

Irish naming traditions are very similar, but as in many Catholic communities, religious and saints' names can come into play as well.

Jewish naming tradition

Like the Yoruba, many Jewish children are named on the eighth day of life. Many are given a religious or traditional name for use in the synagogue, as well as an "everyday" or secular name. Naming your child after ancestors is also quite common, but it is inappropriate for Ashkenazic Jewish children to be named after a still-living relative. However, Sephardic Jewish families will often name their children after living grandparents.

Icelandic naming tradition

Iceland has some very strict rules surrounding how children are named. There is actually a list of names approved by the government. If a parent wishes to go outside this list, they must apply for special approval from a naming committee.

In this situation, there are still criteria that the name must meet in order to be accepted and legalized. The first is that it must make sense in the Icelandic language. The second is that it must be gendered. The third is that it can only contain letters in the Icelandic alphabet.

Afghan naming tradition

Afghans have a unique system for names, in that many do not have surnames. Many given names are just one word, the majority of which are Arabic.

Surnames are becoming more common in Afghanistan, as well as among Afghan families who have immigrated to other countries that legally require a surname. The surname is often chosen based on birthplace or profession. Sometimes family members will have different surnames because of these customs.

Chinese naming tradition

Chinese names follow a two-character system or pattern. The first character is known as the generational name and is shared by all members of a generation. It is placed first as a way to honor the ancestors.

The second character is the child's individual name. Occasionally there is a third character that is also part of the individual name. This individual name is generally symbolic in some way, and relates to specific qualities or traits the family hopes the child will embody.

DNA TESTING

If you are working with blood ancestors, DNA testing can play an essential role in connecting you with both deceased *and* living relatives.

What is DNA?

The abbreviation DNA stands for deoxyribonucleic acid, a special molecule that exists inside and controls every cell of every being on earth. When DNA is "turned on" it creates a special string of code called RNA.

Our DNA is completely unique to us and is made up of 50 percent of our mother's DNA and 50 percent of our father's DNA. It supplies the genetic information for our body, and without it we would not exist.

Understanding how DNA works is an ongoing process, but scientists already know the genetic codes that control many of our physical traits, some inherited, others not.

Even in death, DNA has the capacity to live on. In some cases DNA has been extracted from the corpses of humans and animals that are up to seventy thousand years old—of course, those situations do require specific conditions, but the fact remains that it is still possible.

Recent scientific studies performed on deceased bodies show that some cells and DNA even remain active and change in various ways after death. Understanding this process could lead to exciting developments in the near future in terms of proving the existence of ghosts, spirits, and the afterlife.

Mitochondrial Eve

Did you know that all living humans are descendants of just one human woman? This woman's name is Eve...Mitochondrial Eve.

Mitochondria are tiny cell organs, also called organelles, that produce energy. These organelles have their own specific genome that is passed between females of a species from mother to daughter.

Around two hundred thousand years ago, a time when the world was sparsely populated, Eve was born. There was nothing overtly special about Eve, but she would go on to change the world.

For whatever reason, the other human females existing at the same time as Eve either did not reproduce, or did not produce enough females to keep their mitochondrial genome going, and their maternal lineages ended.

This left Eve as the only surviving maternal ancestor for all of humanity. While other parts of our individual genetic makeup have changed, this one piece of Eve has remained in all of us.

Eve couldn't have known the legacy she would leave behind—she just lived her life the best she could. Her tale is a part of all of us, and it would serve us well to thank her every so often.

History of DNA testing in genetic research and development

Though DNA has been around since the beginning of time, our understanding of it is still relatively new, especially when it comes to using it for the identification of specific people and their relatives; ancestry and ethnicity; and other genetic traits, such as hair and eye color.

Blood type testing: 1900s to 1920s

In 1930 a man named Karl Landsteiner won a Nobel Prize for his 1901 discovery of the reason that a person could accept blood transfusions from one individual successfully while their body would reject other transfusions—often fatally.

Landsteiner theorized that each person had their own blood markers or was part of an identifying group that was compatible with some other groups and incompatible with still others.

In the 1920s, his work was expanded on, and the current red blood typing system of A, AB, B, and O was created. A person's blood type is determined by the blood types of their parents, which, of course, makes it a genetic process powered by DNA.

Serological testing: 1930s to 1970s

Over the next forty years, scientists put much effort into researching how the human body, specifically our blood, works.

This led to the discovery of HLA, or human leukocyte antigen, a protein present in all tissue except for red blood cells. As with the blood type system, people who are not genetically related can share the same HLA type, but when HLA is paired with blood type, scientists can identify genetic relatives with around 80 percent accuracy.

RFLP DNA testing: 1980s

Just ten short years after the discovery of HLA, scientists developed a technique for extracting and testing DNA known as restriction fragment length polymorphism, or RFLP for short.

RFLP was the first test of DNA itself. This is when scientists started to really explore the role DNA plays in the human body, and how it can be used to determine not only paternity but also other familial relationships.

PCR DNA testing: Late 1980s

In the 1980s, polymerase chain reaction (PCR) DNA testing was developed. This technique required only a saliva sample, which was much easier (and faster) to collect than the blood sample needed for RFLP.

SNP DNA testing: 2000s to 2010s

In the early 2000s, DNA changes known as single nucleotide polymorphism, or SNP, could be grouped together to determine factors such as predisposition to diseases and ancestry and ethnicity.

NGS DNA testing: 2010s onward

Since the new millennium, DNA testing has evolved quickly. New discoveries and methods are being created every day. One of these is next generation sequencing, or NGS.

The NGS process takes DNA and RNA and splits them into different groups, sequencing them and then reassembling and analyzing them.

NGS is used for an array of purposes, but one of its main uses is detection of genomic rearrangements (changes in a cell) that cause chromosome issues as well as illnesses such as cancer.

Why have your DNA tested?

DNA advancements haven't just helped the scientific and medical communities, they have also unlocked a wealth of information for the average person.

Today, privately operated companies offer convenient at-home DNA testing kits that anybody can purchase. If you have questions about your background, these tests can help reveal your ethnicity, match you with genetic relatives, aid in records research, and tell you about your genetic health markers.

All you have to do is provide the company with a sample of saliva, register your unique ID, and in six to eight weeks, you will learn what makes you, you.

Pros and cons of DNA testing

Before you begin your journey into the world of DNA testing, it's important to have a clear understanding of potential benefits and repercussions that may arise along the way.

You may discover that your blood relatives are, in fact, not your blood relatives, or are blood relatives, but not in the way you were raised to believe.

Many people have taken DNA tests only to discover that their dad is not their biological father, that they are adopted, or that the people they believe to be their parents are actually their grandparents.

There are many reasons why families lie and keep secrets like this, and most of them come from a place of good intentions.

For some people, discovering that they are adopted can be an amazing and fulfilling experience during which everyone involved embraces the truth; for others, the revelation can be devastating and result in permanently fractured relationships.

And while you may have an idea about how a situation like this would play out in your family, you can never truly be certain until it happens.

DNA testing allows you to connect with genetic relatives.

One invaluable way that DNA tests can be used is to connect you with other genetic family members.

On one hand, these family members may have information pertaining to your ancestors that you would otherwise not be aware of. They may have highly detailed family trees showing multiple generations, or perhaps they have family photos you've never seen.

On the other hand, you may discover that your DNA matches have no further information to offer you. Some may never even respond to inquiries.

And of course, if you're someone who was a genetic surprise, such as a child who was adopted or someone whose paternity was different than expected, you may find yourself rejected and blocked by your new relatives.

Learning about your ethnicity can be both exciting and confusing.

Knowing the history, lore, and geography of your ancestral home is an important part of ancestor work.

Sometimes a person's ancestry is exactly how they expect it to be, but for others, information about their forebears can come as a surprise.

When you first learn your results, you have to understand that they may continue to evolve—as the tests become more and more refined, so do the results.

You must also take care not to appropriate or harm people in your ancestry quest. Just because you have DNA from a certain part of the world or share it with a group of people, you're not automatically entitled to aspects of a culture, especially if you did not grow up in that community.

Every culture is different; some may be open to outsiders, some are open to all people who share their ethnicity, and some are closed completely to outsiders.

These boundaries must always be respected first and foremost.

Ethnicity vs. culture

Ethnicity is your genetic background and shows regions your ancestors lived in for significant periods of time. This is calculated by obtaining DNA samples of people living in that area (and surrounding areas) and then determining the relationship between them. Narrowing down specific regions also requires scientists to study major events and migration patterns of the humans who lived there over thousands of years.

Culture refers to the customs, values, and languages that are exclusive to a particular group of people.

Sometimes ethnicity and culture overlap, and sometimes they do not. One does not automatically entitle you to another.

One final thing to note is that laws surrounding DNA and its collection can be extremely fuzzy and inconsistent. This can be a cause for concern about how your DNA data may be used after you submit it.

DNA testing companies

If you have weighed all the pros and cons of DNA testing and have decided to give it a try, there are two major companies that are worth exploring.

Ancestry

Ancestry is the best-known of the DNA companies, and that is for good reason. Ancestry has been a major player in the genealogical world for many years.

In 1983 the company began by publishing books and magazines about genealogy and ancestry research.

In the 1990s, Ancestry.com was launched, equipped with a computer-based family tree program. By 2001, the company had uploaded and categorized one billion records.

In 2012 they announced their DNA testing kit. The product was a huge success, and in 2014 Ancestry partnered with a great genealogical resource known as FamilySearch to digitize their collection of records.

As of 2022, Ancestry has an impressive thirty billion records available to their members, and over fifteen million DNA tests in their database.

SO WHAT EXACTLY CAN AN ANCESTRY DNA TEST OFFER YOU?

An Ancestry DNA test costs about $100 and will provide you with your ethnicity broken down into genetic percentages, a place to create a family tree, matches with genetic relatives, estimates as to which parts of your ethnicity came from which parent, and, most recently, some genetic health trait testing (a service that will likely be expanded).

If you want to do more with your test results, you will need a membership, which can be a bit on the pricey side. However, if you're looking for your relatives, a membership is well worth the cost, as it grants you access to those thirty billion records. The records come from over eighty countries, and some date as far back as the thirteenth century.

Not only will having all these records available help your research process, but Ancestry also has its own AI technology that will suggest records to you based on your DNA matches and family tree. Of course, it is important to remember that this technology uses the existing data provided by its users, so if someone has made a mistake in their research or family tree, it can mess up the algorithm.

23andMe

While Ancestry took the genealogical and records route, the company 23andMe decided to capitalize on the health aspect of DNA testing.

23andMe was actually the first company to provide the at-home genetic testing model that is so popular today, beginning around 2006–2007.

Their goal was to provide consumers with information about their genetics beyond their ethnicity. They wanted customers to know what genetic variants they carried and what that could mean for their health.

WHAT DOES A 23ANDME DNA TEST OFFER?

23andMe tests range between approximately $100 and $200, depending on which service you choose. They have a basic test that covers ethnicity and reports thirty different traits, and a more complex test that covers ethnicity, reports sixty-five genetic traits, and provides wellness reports and carrier status of genetic anomalies.

Along with these reports, 23andMe provides access to DNA relatives, a place to make a family tree, and the ability to view some historical records.

When it comes to choosing a DNA test for the purpose of ancestor magic, an Ancestry membership is the clear winner. But if you have the funds to take both an Ancestry DNA test and a 23andMe DNA test, it can be interesting to see how the companies' ethnicity estimates compare.

Don't forget to check out the list of resources for searching genealogical records (both free and for purchase) at the back of this book.

Understanding your DNA matches

When I began my ancestor work, I was totally lost. I asked questions such as:

What the hell is a second cousin? (*The child of your parent's first cousin.*)

Is it "grandaunt" or "great-aunt"? (*If they are your grandmother or grandfather's sister, it's grandaunt, not great-aunt. If they are your great-grandmother or great-grandfather's sister, they are your great-grandaunt.*)

How do I figure out who is a cousin twice removed? (*A cousin twice removed is your grandparent's cousin, or your cousin's grandchild or grandparent. To be fair, at this point you aren't that closely linked DNA-wise, with roughly 1.5 percent of shared DNA, versus your first cousin, with whom you share between 7 percent and 13 percent DNA, with 11 percent being average.*)

How are matches determined by DNA tests?

You and your genetic matches are connected through pieces of identical DNA that you all inherited from one or more common ancestors.

DNA tests use a combination of methods to determine matches, but the two terms you should know are "centimorgan" and "segment."

Centimorgan (cM): The unit of frequency with which your DNA overlaps with another person's. The more centimorgans you have in common with another person, the closer you are related genetically. For example, a parent and child will have more centimorgans in common than a niece and aunt.

Segment: All DNA you share with another person is distributed in segments. These segments can be long or short, but the longer ones typically indicate a closer genetic relationship.

When looking through your matches on Ancestry, you will find a list of people who have a predicted relationship to you (such as an aunt or grandchild), the number of centimorgans shared, the number of segments shared, and a percentage estimate of how likely the prediction is to be correct for each match.

Example

Both my father and I have taken tests, and our results on Ancestry look like this:

CLAIRE AND GLEN

> **Shared DNA:** 3,485 cM across 28 segments
> **Longest segment:** 282 cM
>
> **100%** chance of parent-and-child relationship

However, once you look at matches outside your immediate family (parents and full and half siblings), it becomes harder to predict the exact relationship. So in many instances, doing your research is going to be the best way to confirm.

Example

My first cousin on my mother's side and I look like this:

CLAIRE AND ALEXANDRA
>   **Shared DNA:** 727 cM across 28 segments
>   **Longest segment:** 70 cM

87% chance of first-cousin relationship, OR great-grandparent, great-grandchild, grandaunt or granduncle, half aunt or uncle, half niece or half nephew

12% chance of first-cousin-once-removed relationship, OR half first cousin, second great-grandparent, second great-grandchild, second grandaunt or second granduncle, half grandaunt or granduncle, half grandniece or half grandnephew

As you can see, Alexandra and I are most likely first cousins.

If I didn't already know this information, I would determine our relationship by looking at a few documents, such as her public family tree, to determine which ancestors we have in common, or asking her for her date of birth.

Since she is younger than me, it is unlikely (though technically not impossible) that she is my half aunt or half uncle.

And of course, great-grandparent and great-grandchild, as well as grandaunt and granduncle, can be ruled out by virtue of our ages (unless my grandmother's sibling was her parent—again, not impossible, but extremely unlikely).

Why is it difficult to pinpoint DNA outside of immediate family?

Well, even though you inherit half your DNA from each parent, what DNA represents is a random act of nature. Full siblings share 50 percent DNA and have the exact same parents; but which piece of each parent's DNA they inherit and how it is arranged among the others are unique to each sibling.

Basically, genes don't get eliminated, the combinations just vary.

CLANCEY & CO. DNA KITS
MANUFACTURED IN BOSTON

EASY DNA KIT

Manufactured by Clancey & Co.

PATENTED COLLECTION BOTTLE

For instance, I really look like my father's side of the family, and one of my siblings really looks like my mother's side of the family. Chances are our ethnicity percentages would be different as well. While I have 15 percent Balkan in my ancestry, my sister may have 19 percent Balkan in hers, and while I have 45 percent Scottish, she may have 30 percent Scottish, and so on.

Some people are the spitting image of their grandparents, or great-grandparents, or even great-great-grandparents.

I came across a photo of my great-great-great-grandmother Mary, and I was in awe of how much she looked like my father. The resemblance is almost eerie.

What this means is, in terms of the genes that controlled their appearance, my father and his great-great-grandmother happened to have similar combinations of DNA.

As you can see, DNA is really neat, but it isn't the be-all and end-all of ancestor magic. Whom you feel closest to is what's most important in this practice.

CHAPTER SIX

ANCESTOR RESEARCH

Ancestor Research

ANCESTOR RESEARCH AND RECORDS

Record-keeping is an important part of any ancestor practice. It is in records that we learn the identifying details of each individual in our family tree, and this helps us to build the collective history of our family.

Finding records may come easily for some of you, while for others it is a laborious effort resulting in very little "reward." I believe that it isn't the amount of information we find that matters, so much as what we do with what we uncover. If you know ten generations' worth of birth dates but never take the time to honor your ancestors because it is too much work, you're not really cultivating those relationships. Conversely, if you only find two birth dates but make time to celebrate them every year, you may feel a stronger connection to the other side.

Our ancestors' stories are our stories. The lives they lived led to our existence, and having even a basic understanding about who they were can help us feel connected to them—especially those whom we never had the chance to meet.

When you first begin an ancestor practice or a genealogy journey, it can be tempting to just start saving anything and everything you find, but this can create an abundance of problems down the line. Problems such as having the wrong person.

When it comes to record-keeping, you want to think like a detective. If you find a marriage certificate from 1891 that has your great-great-grandmother's name on it, but she was born in 1887...chances are you have the wrong woman. Unless of course she got married at four years of age.

Not only will careless record-keeping screw up your own research, but it can also lead to confusion for the spirits. Names and identities are powerful and work as anchors for those you are trying to attract (page 67).

TIPS FOR RESEARCHING

Begin with one family line, or better yet, with just a few people, preferably those closest to your generation.

Start by researching your grandparents up to five generations. Including aunts and cousins can make things needlessly confusing.

Don't just focus on finding famous or royal ancestors. All of your ancestors are equally important.

And most importantly, break all these rules if that's what feels best for you and your practice.

Now that you have a plan for where to start your research, you may be wondering: What can I do with ancestor records?

IDENTIFICATION

While our ancestors are always around us in spirit, it can be helpful to be able to identify them individually.

Knowing details such as names, birth dates, and death dates can be useful for ancestor spirit communication and other ritual purposes.

Records can also reveal clues about gender identity or sexual orientation. LGBTQ2S people have always existed, and you will have many people in your family tree who are part of that community.

When it comes to identifying lesbian ancestors, start by looking for women who did not marry, or women who did not have custody of their children after a divorce. Being a lesbian was considered a "disorder" in many places such as the British Isles, and therefore custody was almost always awarded to the ex-husband if the woman's identity was discovered.

Identifying gay men can be a little trickier; because male homosexuality was more heavily prosecuted, gay men were more likely to succumb to hetero-normative pressures, but it's not impossible to find them. In these cases the court records and census records will be your best shot.

If your ancestor John Simmons appears as the head of household in multiple census records, and a man named Frank Beauchamp is listed as a boarder in many of them, chances are they were in a committed relationship. This method can be used for lesbian relationships as well.

Trans and nonbinary ancestors are unfortunately a lot harder to track down. Occasionally you may come across newspaper or court accounts of individuals engaging in what would be described as cross-dressing, and those will be the best places to start. If you're extremely fortunate, you may also encounter first-hand accounts in diaries, journals, and letters.

FURTHER THOUGHTS ON RESEARCH

Coming across an interesting or unusual name on a birth register or marriage license can unlock an entire world of knowledge about who your ancestors were.

Like most Eastern Europeans, when my relatives immigrated to Canada in the 1900s, they anglicized their name in order to assimilate better into the dominant culture. When I came across records in Slovakian on Ancestry.com showing my family's original name, it allowed me to narrow down specific neighborhoods in Prešov, Slovakia, and even streets they lived on prior to coming to Canada.

Having a sense of where your ancestors were born and where they lived can teach you about how they may have spent their day-to-day lives. Information such as which jobs they may have performed, what local folktales they might have recited at night to their children, and important food and drink recipes they created can help bring you closer together.

RITUALS AND OFFERINGS

Rituals and offerings are a big part of any ancestor practice, and having a basic understanding of your ancestors' identities can help you tailor your practice to them specifically.

I described my daily candle ritual for ancestors on pages 34–35, and knowing the death dates for your ancestors is a major part of it.

However, time records are just one vector to explore. Research can also help you learn what was grown locally if you want to cook up some ancestral recipes and give them as offerings.

If you are constantly offering alcohol to your ancestors and getting a poor response, records can help you understand why that may be—perhaps religion or addiction history.

THE RECORDS

In the following pages, I will be going over the basic records everybody should look into about their ancestors.

As with all historical documents, you may find it challenging to secure copies of them all. Take your time so that you don't get overwhelmed.

Ancestry records can be found in libraries, government archives, and church archives, as well as on websites such as Ancestry.com and FamilySearch.

Turn to the back of this book for a full list of places to search.

All records should be stored correctly. Never use originals in your BOA. Before you begin, be sure to read the information on pages 137–38 about archiving paper materials.

ENLIST THE LIVING

Before you begin your deep dive into the archives, you should take the time to enlist the help of your living relatives.

You'd be surprised what you can learn by just asking questions.

This is especially important with your older relatives, as they may have answers to questions that cannot be found online. These days you can learn someone's favorite ice cream flavor by just checking Facebook, but that wasn't always the case.

Of course, the first things you should ask about are details that relate to records research. You want to learn as much as you can about names, dates, cemeteries, and schools. After you have as many of those details as possible, you should ask more personal questions.

I have created this list to give you a jumping-off point:

1. What sorts of family traditions did you have growing up?

2. What holidays did your family celebrate?

3. What were your parents' and grandparents' professions?

4. What hobbies did they have?

5. What did your parents and grandparents look like?

6. Do you resemble any family members?

7. Do I resemble any family members?

8. What were their personalities like?

9. What languages did they speak?

10. What was their health like?

11. Did they ever get into any major accidents?

12. Did you have any pets growing up?

13. Did you ever take trips as a family?

14. At what age did you come to this city/town/country?

15. Did your parents or grandparents play sports?

16. Did anyone ever win any competitions?

17. What were your parents' and grandparents' favorite foods, colors, scents, music, or films? (Perfect for offerings.)

18. Did anyone play any musical instruments or have a special skill or talent?

19. What religion were your parents and grandparents?

20. What foods did you eat growing up?

21. Are there any special recipes you can share with me?

22. Did you have a favorite relative?

23. Did anyone have a special nickname?

24. Was anyone LGBTQ2S?

25. What were your parents' and grandparents' marriages like?

26. What inspired your children's names—were they named after anyone?

27. Was anyone adopted or perhaps given up for adoption?

28. What addictions or traumas did your parents or grandparents suffer from?

29. Were there any scandals or secrets you know of?

30. Was anyone's paternity ever disputed?

31. What are your favorite foods, colors, scents, music, or films? (Perfect for offerings.)

32. What do you hope/want to be remembered for?

33. Are there any significant events or memories that stand out?

34. Does anyone have a special marriage proposal story?

35. What was your family's financial situation?

36. What are the family's funerals and memorials like? Are there any special customs?

37. What are your, your parents', and your grandparents' political affiliations?

38. What values and traits do you feel they instilled in you?

39. What was your first job?

DEATH RECORDS

- Death certificates
- Death registers and "Deaths Overseas"
- Cemetery, graveyard, and funeral records
- Obituaries and death notices
- Funeral programs and memorial cards
- Church, synagogue, and parish records
- Coroner and autopsy records
- Wills and probate

When it comes to working with your ancestors' records, you should always begin at the end of their story and work your way backward.

Beginning with someone's death is practical for both spiritual and logistical reasons.

The spiritual reason is that your ancestor practice is about death and honoring those who have passed on. The logistical reason is that death records will contain the most recent data about your ancestors.

Death records are special because they can teach us not only the names and dates of death of our ancestors, but also the names of children, in-laws, and important friends.

Death certificates

A death certificate is a legal document that contains information about a person who has died. Death certificates are used by the family of the deceased or their legal representatives to close down identity-based operations (like bank accounts) via power of attorney, as well as to settle and distribute an estate.

You may find it surprising that death certificates only became standardized in the USA in the 1900s; thus, most death certificates you come across before the twentieth century will be local to a city or township.

Death certificates generally contain a combination of the following criteria: name, address, birth date, death date, known illnesses, education, ethnicity, nationality, marital status, funeral home, burial information, hospital information, and next of kin.

Death registers and "Deaths Overseas"

In most instances, the death records you locate will be what are known as death registers.

A death register is exactly what it sounds like: a record book of deaths from a specific area. Think of this item as the yellow pages of the dead.

In most instances, the death register will contain the person's name, maiden name if applicable, address, cause of death, cemetery or graveyard, a spouse's name, and the physician who tended to them.

In Britain, Canada, and the USA, specific registers known as Deaths Overseas were also kept. The government liked to keep track of anyone who emigrated from their birth country, and of those who traveled a lot, such as sailors and merchants. If you have lost track of an ancestor, try searching for their death overseas.

Cemetery, graveyard, and funeral home records

Cemeteries are one of the best resources for records, as keeping track of where people are buried is necessary in order to place headstones and sell new plots.

However, while good record-keeping is an industry norm, cemeteries aren't immune to lost files or sloppy organization.

Most cities and towns will have what is known as a cemetery trust. Though they are for-profit today, most cemeteries began as city or church-run places, and part of the cemetery trust's job was to keep meticulous records of everybody that passed through the gate.

Prospect Cemetery in Toronto—which is where many of my relatives are buried—is a great example of this trust at work. Each of their records contains name, age, where born, where died, when interred, disease or cause of death, section and lot where the burial plot is located, who owns the plot, medical attendant, officiating minister, undertaker, and any remarks.

In many instances, the funeral home record and the cemetery record will be one and the same, but as our populations have grown, more and more funeral homes have opened, keeping their own records.

Be sure to check out chapter 9, "A Guide to Cemeteries," for more tips about locating your ancestors.

Funeral homes and cemeteries also keep records of cremations, which can be helpful if you haven't found anything by searching for grave sites.

Obituaries and death notices

A death notice is an announcement in a newspaper or online reporting the death of a person. A death notice usually contains a name, details about where the memorial or funeral will be, and what donations can be made on behalf of the family.

An obituary is a biographical entry in a newspaper or online about a person after their death. Historically, obituaries have been reserved for "important people" and are written by newspaper staff.

These days, it is standard practice for a death notice to have some biographical information, and anyone can have one, so don't worry about using the terms interchangeably.

Obituaries and death notices can teach you biographical information about your ancestors that you might not have learned otherwise. Along with names and dates, they also can report milestones or special achievements from the deceased's life.

Likewise, these records can provide you with the information you need to continue your research with funeral home records and cemetery records.

Funeral programs and memorial cards

A funeral program is a pamphlet handed out at a funeral that contains details about the deceased and the order of the service, as well as photos, quotes, poems, and scripture.

Memorial cards are similar to a program but are smaller and contain simple details, such as the deceased's name, a photo, and the date of the funeral. These cards can be passed out at both the wake and the funeral as keepsakes.

In some religious denominations—such as Catholicism—these memorial cards are known as prayer cards and include religious symbols and Bible verses.

Church, synagogue, and parish records

Church and synagogue records are similar to death registers. Most parishes historically kept their own records of congregation and community members who had passed.

Church, synagogue, and parish records generally contain simple details such as name, spouse, and date of death. If a church also runs a graveyard, they will often have a record of where the person was buried.

Coroner and autopsy records

A coroner is a special physician who oversees an autopsy and confirms the details of a person's death. Coroners usually only preside over suspicious or unusual deaths. For run-of-the-mill deaths, a regular doctor or medical examiner will confirm the death.

Coroner records are extremely useful because they can provide a physical description of the person. If you don't have any photos of the ancestor in question, it can be interesting to learn what they looked like as well as any interesting characteristics they may have had.

Coroner records contain information such as medical history, personal effects, address or area the body was brought in from, what method of transport the body arrived in (ambulance, personal vehicle), and, of course, who identified the body.

Wills and probate

A will is a legal document that sets forth instructions about how the deceased wants their estate handled. Funeral and burial instructions are sometimes included, but wills are predominantly used to outline how property will be divided among next of kin. Probate is the legal process of handling and executing the will.

Wills can be a great place to find out information pertaining to spouses and children, as well as any property, business assets, and personal belongings belonging to the deceased.

If you've inherited antiques and heirlooms from your ancestors, perhaps you will see them mentioned in a will!

Because enslaved people were considered property, they are often found in the wills and property records of others. If you have come up against a brick wall in researching enslaved ancestors, this can be an important place to look. Although extremely important, this work can be painful; a team of support, such as a therapist and friends, is a crucial resource for help processing the difficult emotions that can arise while doing this research.

BIRTH RECORDS

- Birth certificates
- Birth registers
- Christening and baptism records
- Birth notices

Birth documents are some of the trickier records to search for from a genealogical standpoint. Infant and child mortality rates were high until recently, and while it may seem cold to us now, people often waited until a child was a little older and past the significant threat of death before recording their birth information. This of course comes with a host of problems, because memories can fade or alter with time.

Another reason that birth records are hard to come by is because most births took place at home rather than in a hospital, so no hospital record was ever created.

Birth certificates

A birth certificate is a legal document that outlines the details of a person's identity, including their name, parents' names, date of birth, and location of birth.

Like death certificates, birth certificates did not become standardized until the twentieth century.

Birth registers

When searching for birth details of an ancestor, you are better off looking through city and town registers.

These registers will contain names, dates (often just the year of birth), parents' names, and addresses.

Christening and baptism records

Churches played a significant role in many of our ancestors' lives and therefore kept records of births as well as baptisms and christenings.

Having your child baptized or christened was extremely important because mortality rates were so high. Parents wanted to ensure that their children would make it to heaven no matter how young they were.

Birth notices

A birth notice is an announcement in a newspaper or online reporting the birth of a person. Birth notices generally contain small snippets of information, such as name, parents' and grandparents' names, date of birth, and location of birth.

Occasionally these notices will also contain a picture of the newborn.

LIFE RECORDS

Now that we have an idea about our ancestors' deaths and our ancestors' births, it's time to figure out what happened in between. This is where what I call life records come into play.

- Censuses
- Marriage and divorce certificates
- Courthouse, police, jail, and other criminal records
- Immigration and travel records
- School records
- Military records
- Occupational records

Censuses

A census is an official government survey of a population that records the details of households and the people who occupy them.

Like death records, genealogists favor censuses because they contain vital information and are updated every few years.

A census may contain all or some of the following information for each member of a given household: names (it always begins with the head of household, who is typically the eldest male), relation to head, address, sex/gender, month of birth, year of birth and age at last birthday, marital status, country or place of birth, year of immigration, year of naturalization, race or ethnicity, nationality, religion, occupation, other employment, employer (or employees if they are the boss), life insurance, and education.

As you can see, the census records of a place are invaluable.

Because birth records are spotty and inconsistent, censuses can also provide information about children.

TIP: In many cases, there are children who are born and then die between census years; see chapter 9, "A Guide to Cemeteries," for more information.

Marriage and divorce certificates

A marriage certificate is a legal document that shows that two people have entered into a marriage contract.

On most marriage certificates, you can find: names of bride and groom; date of the wedding; location; residences and addresses; religious denominations; occupations of both bride and bridegroom; premarital status, such as bachelor, spinster, widower, and widow; names of parents; names of witnesses; and the minister or officiant's name.

A divorce certificate is a legal document that shows that two people have chosen to dissolve their marriage contract.

The information on these certificates is largely the same as on the marriage certificate.

RITUAL IDEA: Print out and frame the marriage certificates of your ancestors and display them somewhere on your own wedding day (or someone's divorce certificate on your divorce day, because sometimes we just need a little extra familial support).

Courthouse, police, jail, and other criminal records

Court records can be a great place to look into your ancestors, and in some instances, you may even come across your ancestors' own words and statements. Court documents are often divided into the following groups: criminal and civil.

These records will have full legal names, birth dates, and addresses, as well as the role your ancestor played in the relevant case: witness, victim, or perpetrator.

In most places, court records are public and can be requested by anyone, but some restrictions do apply on occasion.

Police and jail records aren't always available to the public, as they may contain sensitive information. But more and more government agencies are making these records public after the statute of limitations as well as any copyright dates have passed.

Immigration and travel records

Your ancestor's decision to leave the country they were born in was likely not an easy one. They would have been leaving behind family, friends, and perhaps their native language and customs. Some of your ancestors may have directly participated in the colonization of lands, while others benefited from that colonization years later.

Many would be confined to ships for weeks or months on end, with little more than the clothes on their backs, nervous and excited about what lay waiting on the other side of the journey. Travel and shipping records can also be helpful for locating those who may have been forced to travel against their will, such as enslaved people.

Until recently, when people left their country of origin, they rarely returned. If they left, they would be leaving for good, never to see their loved ones again.

Passports as we know them weren't required until 1920, born out of the desire for countries to remain at peace after the First World War.

Boat passenger lists and other manifests should be the first thing you look through to find ancestors who immigrated to North America, as well as to locate ancestors who *left* North America. These documents often contain the names of everyone traveling as a family unit or group, ages, country of origin and birthplace, and final destination.

Again, immigration records were extremely spotty and did not become standardized until the very late 1800s and early 1900s. If your ancestors immigrated to the United States, be sure to check Canadian records as well. Many people stopped at Canadian ports—particularly in Quebec—before continuing on to their final destination and may appear in those logs.

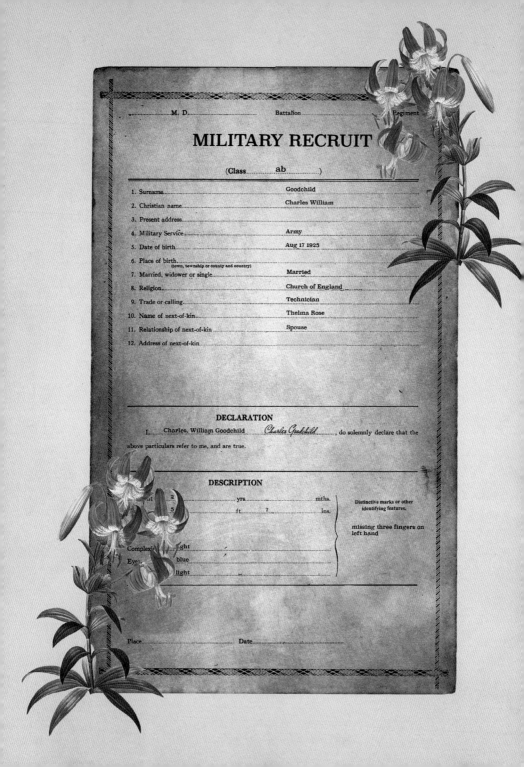

MILITARY RECRUIT

(Class........ **ab** ....)

1. Surname.................... **Goodchild**

2. Christian name.................... **Charles William**

3. Present address....................

4. Military Service.................... **Army**

5. Date of birth.................... **Aug 17 1925**

6. Place of birth....................
   (town, township or county and country)

7. Married, widower or single.................... **Married**

8. Religion.................... **Church of England**

9. Trade or calling.................... **Technician**

10. Name of next-of-kin.................... **Thelma Rose**

11. Relationship of next-of-kin.................... **Spouse**

12. Address of next-of-kin....................

DECLARATION

I, ... Charles, William Goodchild ...... *Charles Goodchild* ......, do solemnly declare that the above particulars refer to me, and are true.

DESCRIPTION

| | 2 | yrs.................... mths. |
| | 5 | ft 7 ins. |

Complexion .... ght

Eyes .... blue

.... light

Distinctive marks or other identifying features.

missing three fingers on left hand

Place.................... Date....................

School records

School registration lists, yearbooks, and alumni lists are a wonderful source of information about your ancestors.

The first official bound yearbook was created at Yale by the class of 1806, and contained information about the students and faculty, but unofficial ones are thought to have existed as early as the 1600s or 1700s.

Alumni lists and records have pretty much existed since the creation of modern institutions. Trinity College in Dublin has been keeping a written record of their students and staff since the sixteenth century.

School records and yearbooks can provide you with information about your ancestors, such as what level of education they reached, what clubs they were members of, and what sports they played.

Military records

Military records are documents kept by each branch of the service with information about all those who served.

These records are invaluable because they sometimes provide descriptive details, such as height, weight, eye color, and hair color, as well as the standard information, such as name, age, spouse, and parents.

Military records can also provide details about an ancestor's death, whether they were missing in action, and whether their body was ever recovered and buried.

However, birth dates on older military and service records should be taken with a grain of salt. Many men would lie about their birth year or month to enlist early—especially in the First and Second World Wars. In fact, my own maternal grandfather enlisted in the navy at seventeen.

Occupational records

Occupational records are those pertaining to your ancestors' work life.

Generally, these details can be found in the census, but some jobs kept their own records.

In the USA, Canada, and Britain, mining and railroad records are widely accessible. When I was looking for a grave for one of my great-great-great-grandfathers, it was a Scottish mining register that informed me he had died in a horrible mine accident. Unfortunately no records of his body being recovered, or where it may have ended up, exist.

Old city directories are another great source of information about your ancestors, and many libraries have scanned and uploaded them online. These directories contained names and addresses of shops and their respective owners.

OTHER RECORDS

- Newspapers
- Photos and albums
- Diaries, journals, and letters

Newspapers
Newspapers are a rich source of information about your ancestors. Articles can lead you to obituaries, court records, and even major city and town events they took part in.

These days, most libraries have major newspapers archived online, available to the public. All it takes to research your ancestors is a few keystrokes and a rough estimate of dates—it's never been easier.

Photos and albums
I discuss photos further in chapter 7, "Heirlooms and Keepsakes," but suffice it to say that photos are a great resource for ancestry research. If you are lucky enough to have photos of your family, not only will you have the opportunity to see what they looked like, but you may also learn about other ancestors you had not known existed.

Diaries, journals, and letters
Nothing is more valuable in the research process than written accounts from your ancestors themselves.

THE DAILY SPIRITUALIST

Issue No. 346   ILLUSTRATED NEWS   Nov 16, 1898

Dead at t

The most terrible of all the collision was over in the e
press engine   of the
engineer of the   Wm. H.
Brady, and John   his fireman, were found   by under
heaps of wreckage and the fireman's
body, being pressed against the fire-box,
was literally cooked. Both men had
evidently stuck to their posts up to the
time of the collision and both probably
met death at the same moment. As the
fire was at its   passed and
the bodies were not been buried to the
locality

WERE KILLED

Accident on the
and Trunk Railway.

THE DEAD.

Charles Goodchild, drover, Beaton
Toronto.

drover and butcher,
Toronto.

rand Trunk Railway
ooksville.

John Mcdonald, Grand Trunk fireman Belleville.

William Brady, Grand Trunk engineer, Belleville.

Hector C. Ross, Russian immigrant.
Olga Halfrid, Russian immigrant.
Marina, Russian traveller immi-
grant.

W   of passenger
train   brought
Walker   peacefully and
ewstood with placid visage. His engi-
neman   mer, who
was a king of touching him on the
engine, the two stiles died, was
almost denth in particularly pathetic. He is
an old employee of the Grand Trunk,
having been on the service some 25
years. This morning he was on his
way to Whitby Junction with Walker
his fireman to take charge of an engine. Casey has a wife and several children and leaves a splendid reputation as
a careful and painstaking engineer.
The news agent on the train had a
narrow escape but was slightly injured.
It is earned a great deal of praise by
an energetic effort in the rescue corps.

ing for the express   on the rear
board she took   apprehended on the line
from and severe wounds think prod
being
from
prefer
compa
the fa
the Ta

T

Not only will personal papers provide firsthand accounts of their lives, but you will also be holding something sacred they put a lot of energy into. A major part of witchcraft is about focusing or channeling your intent. The time, energy, and emotions your ancestors put into writing their experiences down present a powerful example of this process.

BRICK WALLS

During your ancestor research, there will be many times when you'll come up against what are known as brick walls.

Brick walls are dead ends that stall your progress. These can be frustrating and sometimes even make you want to give up your search altogether.

Below are some tips and ideas to help you break through these walls.

Try alternate spellings of names

As I mentioned earlier about my Slovakian ancestors, names were often anglicized to help people blend in. Other times, a wall can arise when a census worker misrecorded something. Two of my ancestors' maiden names appear differently in almost every record. One is Luesby, but it is often written as Luseby, and another is Hemmaway, but it is often rendered as Hemmerway.

Broaden your birth and death dates

There are many reasons why birth years and even death years can be wrong. Sometimes people didn't even know what month they were born in. Try adding or subtracting a couple of years when researching and even including the month before and after their supposed birth date.

No records for enslaved people

When researching enslaved ancestors, the brick walls can be endless. For centuries, these men and women were not recognized as people and were therefore not recorded other than in property records. Many Black Americans will find it helpful to begin with the post–Civil War census of 1870 and work backward and forward from there.

Many enslaved people relocated to the Northern states as well as into Canada, so be sure to check these records as well.

See the back of this book for a list of resources that are geared specifically toward African ancestry research in Canada and the USA.

No records for Indigenous and First Nations people

Many Indigenous men and women were also kidnapped and forced into slavery, as well as forced to suffer through the abuse and genocide of the residential school system in Canada and the USA.

Entire tribes, languages, and cultures were purposefully erased, horrors that are still ongoing even today.

The Government of Canada and First Nations task forces have set up specific archives to help people trace their families. If you are unsure of where to begin, try reaching out to your local library, as they may have a list of organizations you can contact.

See the list of resources at the back of this book that are geared specifically toward Indigenous ancestry research in Canada and the USA.

Poverty, addiction, and homelessness

An unfortunate reality of genealogy is realizing that sometimes your ancestors can't be found because they were too poor or unwell to be considered important enough for the common records.

If someone is missing or there are large gaps in reports like the census, try looking in church, workhouse, and other institutional records.

There may be times when you just need to accept that you cannot go any further in your research. This doesn't mean that you can't cultivate a fulfilling spiritual relationship with your ancestors.

RITUAL: WRITE A EULOGY

Once you have gathered enough information about your ancestors, you may wish to write and read a eulogy for one (or all) of them.

A eulogy is a speech made in tribute to a deceased person. The eulogy highlights details about the deceased's life and is an important part of a funeral or memorial service, for both the living and the dead.

When you take the time to write a eulogy for someone, you are showing how much you care for them (even if you never met). It can be a great bonding experience for you and the spirits, and can teach future generations details about the person.

I wrote and recited my first eulogy at ten years old for my paternal grandmother, Thelma Rose. Even at that age, I knew it was important that one of her five grandchildren speak on behalf of the group and show all the mourners how special she was to us.

Nana was the dear grandma of Hayley, myself Claire, Monica, Justine, and Genrys Goodchild. She never missed a birthday, Christmas, etc. She was nice to all of us. Whenever we went to her apartment, she would give us something to eat and drink. She had a photo album for all of us. She wrote our names on the top and inside what number we were born.

She even had a wedding album for my parents. Nana also had one for my aunt and uncle.

I remember when Nana got her two cats Misty and Stormy. If my dad and uncle can't find a home for them, we might get one.

All of the grandchildren love and miss her very much.

After I finished *The Book of Séances*, I wrote another eulogy for her as a thank-you for all the help and guidance she gave me in completing sections of that book:

Thelma, or Nana as I called her, was one of those special people. The kind who made the world a better place just because she was in it. Soft-spoken, sweet, and compassionate, Thelma was cherished by everyone who knew her.

Family was incredibly important to her, and she made sure we all knew it. When your birthday or another special holiday rolled around, you could be certain that the first phone call of the day would be from her.

Though my memories of her from when she was alive are few in number, those I do have will remain with me for the rest of my life. And even though she is gone from the physical world, I am grateful that she is a constant presence in my life through spirit work.

Since Nana is an active spiritual guide for me, I am blessed with the ability to make new memories with her and turn to her for advice. She proved instrumental in helping me to complete a chapter of The Book of Séances, *as well as guiding me through tumultuous times over the last few years, and for that I will be forever grateful.*

These eulogies should go in your BOA and can also be incorporated into the daily candle ritual in chapter 3.

ACT OF SERVICE: PHOTO-SHARING BLOG

One wonderful way to give back to both the ancestor and the genealogical communities is by creating a photo-sharing blog or website.

There will be many instances throughout this process in which you come across photos of not only your ancestors, but other people's as well.

What better way to help someone else than to share what you have discovered?

If you have physical photos, you will already be scanning them to use for your BOA or personal records (we never use originals for this—look to chapter 7, "Heirlooms and Keepsakes," for the reason), so why not add one more simple step and upload them to a website with any identifying information?

If you know any of the following, be sure to include it with the photo: name, date, location, inherited from, located at, etc.

When I was writing *The Book of Séances*, I came across a postcard that had a portrait photo of a medium from the nineteenth century. I felt oddly drawn to it, so I purchased it for a couple of dollars and added it to my collection of antique ephemera.

One afternoon a few months later I was chatting with one of my customers, Nina, and a few other people when she mentioned being related to this medium.

I didn't mention the image, but I did let her know I had come across her relative during my research.

That evening I slipped the postcard into an envelope and sent it on its way to Nina.

I believe Nina's ancestor knew I was connected with her, and that is why I felt the compulsion to acquire it.

Something that cost me very little ended up being extremely valuable to Nina and her ancestor journey.

ACT OF SERVICE: HEAD TO THE ARCHIVES

People are moving farther away than ever from their hometowns and countries of origin. And while there are many benefits to starting over somewhere new, it does make accessing historical records somewhat tricky.

If you are part of a genealogical group or other such organization online, let others know you are available to help search the archives and reference libraries closest to you.

Nothing feels worse than coming across a record online only to find out it can only be viewed in person and to realize you have no way of getting there.

Remember that when doing research for others, you need to ensure that you document all the information on the record completely. What feels irrelevant to you may be vital to someone else.

CHAPTER SEVEN

HEIRLOOMS AND KEEPSAKES

7

Heirlooms and Keepsakes

Heirlooms and keepsakes are the physical history of our more recent ancestors. When their lives have ended and their bodies have returned to the earth, it is these objects that we hold on to in order to keep their memory alive.

When you hold the pocket watch that your father carried every day, you are transported to another place and time, when he was still a living, breathing person.

In this situation, not only are *you* transported, but your father's spirit is as well, since heirlooms and keepsakes make extremely powerful spirit anchors.

But what exactly are heirlooms and keepsakes?

An **heirloom** is an item of monetary value that has been passed down through a family for generations.

A **keepsake** is an item of sentimental value that has been passed down through a family for generations.

Most people use the terms interchangeably (myself included), but it's helpful to know the difference when doing research and documenting them for your BOA.

When you are building your ancestor practice, heirlooms can be instrumental in helping to forge a strong spiritual connection with your loved ones. Heirlooms foster this connection through emotions and memories, but they can also teach you about your ancestors—especially about those who died before you were born.

These objects can reveal a lot, if you know what to look for.

The easiest thing to decipher from an heirloom or keepsake is the socio-economic status of your loved one. For example, the number of luxury items, like jewelry and photographs, can reveal whether or not that person had disposable income.

The condition of an heirloom can also give you a glimpse into how much money someone earned. An item that shows signs of wear or has been repaired multiple times can mean there were no funds to replace it.

Heirlooms and keepsakes can also reveal hobbies, interests, and even professions. If you find an old baseball in a box of your uncle George's things, a quick Google search can lead you to articles about the time he spent playing in the minor leagues.

Take a minute to think about the items you have inherited from your loved ones. What do they say about your family? Were they weird or creative in some way? Maybe they were classic and understated? Do you have many items from them or just a few?

Write down the story these items tell in your BOA.

Next, think about your own cherished possessions. Are they clearly on display in your home, or are they tucked away somewhere safe? What do these items say about you?

CARING FOR HEIRLOOMS

The first thing you must do is inventory the heirlooms and keepsakes you have inherited.

Dedicate a section of your BOA to this task.

Each item should have a written record and a photograph. You can find record templates for common heirlooms throughout this chapter. Feel free to modify them to suit your needs.

Evaluate the state of each item. Is it in good condition? Does something need repairs? If something is beyond saving, can just a piece of it be kept?

If you make the decision to get rid of something, be sure to document it first (include a photograph) and write down where it has gone. Your heirs will thank you when they don't need to search for hours for an item that was given away thirty years earlier.

While most items like jewelry and furniture are relatively safe out in the open, paper and fabric require special care when it comes to safekeeping and storage.

Paper

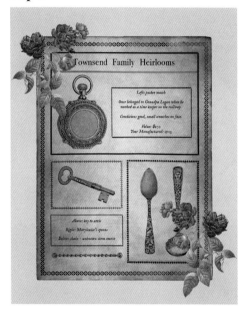

Paper is probably the most valuable item you will inherit. Paper covers birth certificates, marriage licenses, funeral ephemera, diaries, cookbooks, and photos.

Always remember when handling these precious documents: Unless someone before you has taken the time to make copies, you are probably holding the only ones in existence.

The first step is acquiring proper archival supplies. Paper must be stored in acid-free, lignin-free, pH-neutral envelopes and storage boxes.

This can be a bit of a financial investment, so if the items are recently inherited, the conservator or the executor of the estate may be able to allocate funds to help you with the cost.

Pro tip: Start your own fund of around $1,000 to go toward heirloom storage and repairs for your own descendants. While that amount isn't feasible for everyone in one go, putting a couple of dollars a month into a secure savings account can add up over the years.

Determining the categories into which to sort your heirlooms is a matter of preference. Some prefer to organize by type (such as all birth certificates together), while others like to group by each individual ancestor.

After you've done your categorizing, every item must be scanned.

While this process can be tedious, remember that you are helping future generations by doing this.

Be sure to back up your scans in three separate locations. The first should be a cloud-based storage service; the second is a copy emailed to yourself; and the third is a physical zip drive.

> Pro tip: For the first two backup methods, try using two different log-in details just in case you lose access to one.

After this process is complete, the originals should be archived correctly using the storage supplies you purchased. Keep them away from dampness and excessive temperature changes.

> Pro tip: Newspapers should only be stored with other newspapers. The chemicals they contain will destroy other items over time.

Use printed copies of all these paper items for your BOA. Don't forget to write down where the originals are kept! Fireproof safes and safety-deposit boxes are great tools if you have the means to pay for them. Be sure to leave keys, codes, and passwords somewhere accessible so future generations can access the originals and the backups.

Fabric

Fabric items are some of the most common heirlooms, as well as some of the most difficult to preserve and to store.

Though today we overconsume clothing and other textiles, it wasn't that long ago that our most valuable items were passed down and used by the next generation. Almost everyone has a memory of wearing hand-me-downs.

Fabric heirlooms can include baby blankets, quilts, tablecloths, uniforms, wedding attire, and embroidery.

For each item you receive, you should take a photograph and provide a written description.

Unlike paper items and records in which all the information is often recorded on the actual item, clothing and textiles may require you to fill in the details.

Who wore it and why? How many generations have owned it?

As with paper, all your fabric storage materials should be acid-free and dye-free.

Fabric should be folded or laid flat in a box, covered with tissue paper, and—if you can—placed in a cedar chest to deter moths. Cedar chips can also be purchased from a plant nursery as well as big-box stores and specialty craft stores. I recommend keeping those in a plastic bag with some holes poked in it (to avoid having the chips rub against your clothing and discolor it).

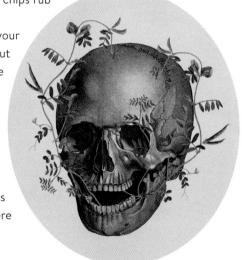

If you'd like to display some of your fabric items, be sure to keep them out of direct sunlight or they can become bleached or faded.

Needlework and smaller items look best framed and hung on a wall. Always use UV-protective glass when framing your heirlooms and keepsakes.

Again, be sure to leave instructions and records in your BOA about where these items are located.

COMMON HEIRLOOMS AND WHAT TO DO WITH THEM

Jewelry

Thanks to the combination of monetary value and sentimentality, jewelry tops the list as the most common family heirloom. Even costume jewelry that may not have been very expensive during its time tends to appreciate in value over the years. And even if that's not the case, there is probably still a good reason it was kept and passed down.

Engagement rings, wedding bands, charm bracelets, and lockets are the most common jewelry items handed down through a family, and receiving one of these is a huge honor.

The most important thing to do when you inherit jewelry is to learn and document its backstory in your BOA so future generations know its importance.

A gold wedding band may appear to be just an ordinary token of love, but it could have an exciting or heartwarming history attached to it.

When my partner's father was first battling terminal cancer, my partner took over a lot of the activities his father could no longer do.

One day, while digging in the back garden, my partner came across a gold wedding band deep in the earth.

It turns out his father had lost his original wedding ring in the garden twenty years before and had to replace it.

In the four years I've known him, I've never seen my partner without that ring on his finger. Every time he looks down at it, he feels a connection to his father's spirit.

Heirloom Jewelry Record

Physical description/Photo:

Material/Metal:

Value:

History:

Inherited from:

Inherited by:

Feel free to amend these record prompts to suit your personal needs.

Using heirloom jewelry in magic

PROTECTIVE AMULET

An amulet is a piece of jewelry worn to protect the wearer from danger, illness, or other malevolent forces.

It is in your ancestor's best interests that you survive and thrive; therefore, using an item of their jewelry as a protective amulet is a good idea—especially when engaging in spellwork or visiting high-energy places, such as a cemetery.

PENDULUM

If divination is something you engage in with your ancestors, using a piece of jewelry as a pendulum is a wonderful idea.

A pendulum is a weighted object attached to a cord that is used for answering yes-or-no questions. The cord or chain is held in one hand and the weighted item is suspended in the air. When you ask a question, the weight swings in one direction for yes and another for no.

Making a Pendulum

What you need

A ring or pendant.

A piece of red cord or string about 8 inches
long. Embroidery floss works best.

Take your red cord (which represents the bloodline) and tie one end to the ring or pendant...and you're done!

Making a pendulum is an incredibly easy thing to do.

Mastering its use...well...that's a different story.

If you want to experiment using different-color threads, use the chart on page 267 to help you choose the right color.

Timepieces

A timepiece is an instrument used for telling time. There are two main types: watches and clocks. A watch is a small, portable timepiece that is carried or worn. A clock is a nonportable timepiece that is typically mounted on a wall but can also stand on furniture or the floor.

The two most popular kinds of timepieces handed down as heirlooms are grandfather clocks and pocket watches.

The grandfather clock, more formally called the long-case clock, was created in 1656 when a Dutch inventor first used a weighted pendulum (not the divination kind) inside a clock. Over the years, the design was perfected by English craftsmen, and these clocks have been a staple in many homes since.

So how did the long-case clock get its better-known pseudonym, the grandfather clock? In 1875, a songwriter named Henry Clay Work was visiting England from America. Work was staying at the George Hotel in Yorkshire, where he noticed a large long-case clock in the lobby that wasn't keeping time. When he inquired about it, he was told the following tale.

The clock had belonged to the previous hotel owners, two men known as the Jenkins brothers.

During their lives, the clock had always kept time perfectly, but when one of the brothers died, the clock slowly started falling out of sync.

When the second brother died, the clock stopped working altogether.

A repairman was called, but nobody could find the cause of the problem, and the clock had been left unworking since.

So inspired by the story was Henry Clay Work that he wrote a song about it called "My Grandfather's Clock," and the rest is history.

The portable watch was invented by a German man named Peter Henlein in the sixteenth century. The idea of a portable timepiece was very popular, and his design was worn around the neck by the upper echelon of society.

Over the next three hundred years, the watch went through many changes. The design was simplified, and in the 1800s the watch moved from the neck to the vest pocket (though some people had already taken to keeping it in their pocket). This is where the term "pocket watch" originates.

Pocket watches were a staple in men's fashion until World War I. Soldiers

found them cumbersome to carry in battle and switched to the simpler wrist-watch.

Despite their dip in popularity, pocket watches were still worn well into the 1970s.

Pocket watches are most often passed down from father to son, but these days they can be enjoyed by everyone regardless of gender identity.

Heirloom Timepiece Record

Physical description/Photo:

Type (clock or watch):

Value:

History:

Inherited from:

Inherited by:

Using heirloom timepieces in magic

The clock is one of the oldest symbols of mortality there is. Clocks represent the fact that every person has a finite number of minutes here on earth, and nobody can evade death when that number is up.

PROTECTIVE AMULET

Like jewelry, using a pocket watch as an amulet for protection is a great idea, especially if you are traveling by train (pocket watches were a staple for employees of the railroads for many years).

In February 1872, the head engineer of the Canadian Pacific Railway proposed the concept of World Wide Standard Time, though encouraging all the other railways to switch over to this system would take years of persistence.

By November 1883, most of the railways in the USA and Canada had switched from using more than six hundred different schedules to using just four time zones: Eastern, Central, Mountain, and Pacific.

In April 1891, near Cleveland, Ohio, an accident took place that would solidify the need for proper timekeeping and careful inspection of workers' watches in the railroad industry.

Two trains collided at devastating speeds because one conductor had failed to realize that his watch was running a few minutes behind. The mistake was fatal, taking nine lives.

After this crash, watches were heavily regulated and inspected by a special railroad timekeeper every single day. Your pocket watch had to be manufactured to certain specifications, and if you forgot it, you were out of a job.

If you don't feel comfortable carrying an heirloom pocket watch on vacation (and I wouldn't blame you if you didn't), try placing it on your ancestor altar for the duration of your trip. Ask your ancestors to ensure that all vehicles are running on schedule, and that you will return unaffected by delays and accidents.

This exercise can also be performed using a clock. If yours is too large to sit on your altar, you can write down your wishes on a piece of paper and slip it inside the clock or attach it to the bottom or back using a nondamaging adhesive (such as painter's tape).

Furniture

One of the most common, and least-wanted, kinds of heirlooms is furniture.

As apartments and living spaces become smaller, people have less room for inherited furniture. Still, family furnishings can be among the most important heirlooms we can receive, especially if we come from a family that isn't wealthy—which is most of us.

In such instances, furniture takes on an even bigger meaning.

There are probably pieces that have been shared by multiple generations in your family. Perhaps the desk your mother writes at was once her great-aunt's kitchen table...and before that, it was owned by that person's godmother.

Furniture holds so much importance and so much energy. It is witness to countless memories, family gatherings, births, deaths, and everything in between.

Before the advent of cheap DIY furniture, items were usually made by skilled artisans. Even if something was made by an ordinary person, it was still composed of solid materials, not particleboard and cheap veneer.

Heirloom Furniture Record

Physical description/Photo:

Type (desk, bed, etc.):

Value:

History:

Inherited from:

Inherited by:

Using heirloom furniture in magic

The most obvious and useful way to incorporate furniture into your practice is by using a piece as your ancestor altar (pages 68–69).

Items like desks, bookshelves, and nightstands are all great for this purpose, but don't be afraid to get creative. I know someone who used old boards from a barn on the family farm to make a set of shelves that now holds all their other heirlooms.

If furniture you inherit is in such bad condition that you need to get rid of it, consider keeping a piece of the original and placing it on or near your altar to serve as an anchor. For example, you could cut a heart shape out of a desk or table, or fill a jar with nails and screws from an old rocking chair. In this instance, it's less about aesthetics and more about holding on to the spiritual energy in the item.

If you do decide to part with a piece of furniture, be sure to photograph and log the piece first. Write down where it was donated or whom it was given to.

Pottery, china, and crystal

Twenty or thirty years ago, inheriting a set of china dishes or a crystal vase was an honor for most people, but today we can't seem to get rid of old china fast enough. Enter any charity shop and you will see rows and rows of teacups, saucers, and other serving dishes. A veritable graveyard of wedding china and anniversary gifts.

Why we are so eager to rid ourselves of pottery and similar items baffles me.

Pottery is a powerful link to our recent ancestors, but also to our ancient ones.

When an archeologist digs in a location and comes across a broken pot, they don't shrug and toss it aside, saying, "Oh, great, another fragment of a pot." No, they marvel at it. From an archeological standpoint, a piece of pottery is worth more than all the gold in the world. Pottery equals community. It means people lived, ate, slept, and even died in the place where it was discovered. That fragment represents our humanity.

When you have a chance to inherit china, crystal, or pottery, take it and cherish it. Know that when you hold it, you are connected to a lineage that spans all of history.

Heirloom Pottery Record

Physical description/Photo:

Type (cup, crystal, etc.):

Value:

History:

Inherited from:

Inherited by:

Using heirloom pottery, china, and crystal in magic

OFFERINGS

If you are lucky enough to inherit teacups and other drinking vessels, my first suggestion would be to use them for offerings. Drinks in favorite mugs and teacups will always be appreciated by an ancestor. Food offerings on wedding china could mean a lot to, say, your parents, if their marriage always inspired you.

The same can be said for vases and other decorative dishes. They are perfect for holding flower offerings, food, and other trinkets.

DIVINATION

Teacups can also be used for divination! In *The Book of Séances* I wrote about the collection of teacups my paternal grandmother had and how they were instrumental to my tea-leaf-reading journey.

Tea-leaf reading can be a wonderful way to bond with your ancestors and reveal clues about their lives through symbols.

ALTAR DECORATION

Another fun way to repurpose dishes like plates is to add a hook to the back of each one and hang them on the wall around your ancestor altar. If you have an entire set, you could make one for each family member as a gift (just make sure to note in your BOA who received each one).

Quilts and textiles

As you learned at the beginning of this chapter, inheriting quilts and other textiles is tricky because in most cases they need to be stored just right or they will disintegrate over time.

Creating textiles is something found across all cultures on earth. Each country may have their own colors, patterns, and techniques, but like making pottery, weaving and sewing are activities shared by all humans.

Clothing and blankets provide us with warmth, safety, and security. Clothing can tell the world of your profession and your favorite color, and can be a way to express your personality. There is a special kind of magic in textiles because of how much they communicate to the outside world.

Clothing has also been used to show when someone is in mourning.

In the Victorian era, there was a strict code women were expected to follow in terms of dress and jewelry. When a woman was grieving the death of a spouse, she wore black clothing, jewelry, and special capes and veils for two years, though grays and lavenders were allowed in small amounts during the last six months of this mandatory mourning period. Men had far fewer rules to obey and could usually get away with a dark-colored suit for a few months.

Sewing and weaving have always been predominantly female crafts and professions, and the majority of textile artisans today are still women.

Throughout history, multiple generations of women in a family or community could be found gathered in rooms to take part in the creation of fabric. It was in these rooms and in sacred weaving circles where folklore, memories, and family history would be shared. Lessons in patterns and technique were passed from grandmother to granddaughter, family secrets only perfected through years of practice.

Of course, not every item of clothing or fabric you inherit will be handmade, but such items still represent these traditions and can have powerful stories attached to them.

Imagine how much feeling and energy must be woven into the fabric of a wedding dress or military uniform. A simple blanket can contain the memory of long, cold winter nights, and a plain collared shirt can be the keeper of first-day-of-school jitters.

Heirloom Textile Record

Physical description/Photo:

Type (dress, blanket, etc.):

Value:

History:

Inherited from:

Inherited by:

Using textiles in magic

Weaving and the use of thread are highly symbolic of life, death, and the fate of each human. Stories surrounding thread, yarn, and weaving appear in Greek, Norse, Egyptian, and Chinese myths, as well as countless others.

EMBROIDERY

A common tool in traditional and folk witchcraft is the red thread. The red thread represents the actual bloodline of your family, as well as the metaphorical bloodline shared by all witches.

One easy way to incorporate the red thread and give your fabric heirloom a bit more oomph is to embroider your family name or different sigils into a corner of the cloth. Sewing names into fabric was a common tradition well into the 1980s.

Remember that a name contains power—see pages 92–96.

WITCHES' LADDER

Threads, cords, and strings are used to make witches' ladders and in other types of knot magic.

The term "witches' ladder" was first used in 1879 in Somerset, England, when one of these string charms was found in the attic of a home. This charm consisted of one long cord with various knots tied throughout it, each one holding a feather.

These charms were likely used for a number of purposes, from protection to cursing.

These days they are used predominantly for protecting one's self or home.

Items of clothing or fabric that are in poor condition can be easily repurposed for these forms of magic.

If you want to make a witches' ladder out of an old garment, the first step is making a rope.

Cut the fabric into strips that are between ¼ inch and 1 inch wide. Length can vary, but 6 to 8 inches will work best.

First, tie two of the strips together at one end. Then take one of the strips and spin it a few times in an outward motion. Think of it like curling hair in a curling iron. You're making each piece into a coil. Then take the other strip and do the same. Next, you want to wrap these coils around each other tightly. By spinning each strip of fabric on its own first, you're giving it a bit of texture and strength. It will naturally want to pull back on itself, which helps tighten your rope. Continue working with the strips until you've reached about ¼ inch from the bottom and tie a knot to secure them.

If you find this process difficult, you can take three scraps of fabric and braid them together instead.

The next step is to gather your ladder "rungs." These can be anything you'd like. Feathers are traditional, but some people use metal charms, crystals, or bones.

Tie each rung into place, evenly spaced, by making knots along your rope. As you do this, think about your room filling with a protective and calming energy.

When it's finished, hang the witches' ladder above your ancestor altar or by your front door.

ALTAR CLOTHS

If you have inherited items like tablecloths and runners and don't want to keep them tucked away, the most obvious choice is to turn them into altar cloths for your ancestor altar. Altar cloths are common in both witchcraft and mainstream religions and are protective and spiritual in nature.

ADDING SQUARES TO A QUILT

If you were lucky enough to inherit a family quilt, don't be afraid to add your own squares or details. Each square or section represents a person and their story in the family, and this includes you!

As you add your own touch to your quilt, think about what message you want to send to future generations. Envision your ancestors—both old and new—holding their hands over yours as you place each thread.

GOOD-LUCK CHARMS

Another form of simple textile magic that doesn't involve any alteration is the practice of displaying certain items on specific days.

Your mother's wedding dress can be placed in your dressing room on your own wedding day and act as your "something old."

One of your dad's Cub Scout badges can be a good-luck charm for when you are embarking on a travel adventure or learning a new skill.

Recipes and cookbooks

Heirloom Recipe Record

Follow the preservation steps for paper records on pages 137–38.

Physical description/Photo:

Type (recipe, cookbook, etc.):

History:

Inherited from:

Inherited by:

Recipes and family cookbooks represent the heart and soul of a home: the kitchen.

The kitchen is where people come together, whether it is for a simple breakfast of oatmeal or an elaborate holiday feast consisting of fifteen different dishes.

Recipes have always been an integral part of human history. Even while our species were still hunter-gatherers, recipes played a role. Which plants and animals were edible and how to prepare them were taught (orally) by one generation to the next. This information was crucial for survival.

According to most archeologists and paleontologists, our earliest human ancestors probably began using fire to cook about four hundred thousand years ago.

Then around twelve thousand years ago, agriculture developed in the area of the Middle East known as the Fertile Crescent. About five thousand years ago, writing was invented in Mesopotamia in the form of cuneiform, and with those tablets came the first written recipes!

Most families, if not all, have at least one secret recipe or tradition. If you've ever been privy to yours, you know it can feel like joining an exclusive club.

Inheriting recipe cards or cookbooks is like inheriting sacred knowledge.

Cooking these meals is comforting to both you and your ancestors and should be done often.

Using recipes in magic

HOST A DINNER

Every Samhain (Halloween), I host a potluck for my sisters, my cousins, and their partners. We are each required to cook a recipe that has ties to our family or cultural identity.

Before they arrive, I invite all our ancestors to join us that evening for the meal. Everyone (living and dead) always has a great time. Hosting one of these dinners yourself is the perfect way to share one of the recipes you have inherited.

If you decide to host an ancestor dinner, be sure to get a copy of the recipe each person brought and include them all in your BOA with details about who brought what and why. Make copies of all the recipes for each attendee as well so they can enjoy them at home.

PERFORM A BONDING ACTIVITY

If hosting an elaborate dinner isn't your thing, you can still make recipes for your ancestors as offerings. Your aunt's spirit will enjoy spending time with you in the kitchen baking cookies just as much as you will enjoy eating them afterward.

You may wish to try cooking a recipe specifically for your ancient ancestors as well. Show them how far we have come in terms of ingredients and cooking utensils. With a little research and creativity, you can give an ancient dish a modern twist.

Photos and albums

What a magnificent gift it is to inherit photos and photo albums.

We take photography for granted now because we each carry a camera in our pocket every day, but once upon a time, photographs were among a person's most prized possessions.

Photography as we know it was not invented until 1839, so these heirlooms have only existed for a relatively short period of time, which adds immense sentimental and monetary value to them.

As people began migrating around the world, a photograph often became the only connection they had to their family and their homeland.

Having a photograph gave people the opportunity to at least look at their loved ones when they missed them or felt homesick.

Some people would spend three to six months' salary on a single photo, but it was worth it to them to create that connection.

Of course, most people in those early days of photography could never afford a photograph. There are people in my paternal family tree whom I will never see because they were too poor to have portraits taken. This is the reality for most of us, so if you do happen to have an ancestor photo in your possession, cherish it. You also have a responsibility to put that photo online. Make uploading it to a website like Ancestry.com your number one priority so that your other relatives and ancestors can have the opportunity to see their family members as well.

Photo and Album Record

Follow the preservation steps for paper records on pages 137–38.

Physical description and copy of photo:

Who is in it:

Personal history:

Photo type (daguerreotype, ambrotype, etc.):

Inherited from:

Inherited by:

Using photos in magic

DISPLAY

The most powerful magic you can do with a photo is to just appreciate it and put it on display (a copy, not the original, please). Looking into the faces of your ancestors builds a wonderful connection between you.

While I encourage you to put copies of these photos in your BOA (chapter 2) and on your ancestor altar (chapter 4), I feel it is important to include a more in-depth ritual for turning photos into magical protection items.

What you need

- High-quality copies of the photos (I recommend hiring a professional service to print them for you)
- A red marker
- Picture frames (bonus points if these were inherited or crafted out of old furniture)
- Sheets of paper smaller than the photos

For each photo, record the following in red marker on a piece of paper: "[Name(s)], I ask that you watch over me and my home with love and with protection. May negative energy and negative people be stopped in their tracks."

Place the paper in the frame and lay the photo over it. Hang these photos by your altar or in various places around your home. Hanging them over your front door is a great way for your ancestors' spirits to assess who is coming into your home.

WHEN YOU HAVEN'T INHERITED ANYTHING...

You may be sitting there reading this chapter and wondering if it applies to you because you didn't inherit any heirlooms. Of course it does!

I understand that it can be painful not to have the special items that others do. There are lots of reasons why you may not have inherited anything. Your ancestors' possessions may have been lost, stolen, or destroyed; you may be estranged from your immediate family without access to them; or items may simply have gone to a different family member.

There are still ways to incorporate what you do have, and that is what you will learn in this section of the chapter.

Heirlooms of connection

Heirlooms of connection are items that weren't actually owned by your ancestors, but which are brought into your practice to represent them.

They are symbolic of the person as well as your relationship to them. Many of your ancestor altar objects and decorations can likely be placed in this category as well.

The first step in working with heirlooms of connection is research. Think like a detective or FBI profiler. Go through all the records and photographs you have gathered about your ancestors (chapter 6). What can you discern from these? Try looking into the area where they lived or their country of origin to help put together a broader picture of what they may have eaten, worn, or celebrated.

The heirlooms of connection you choose will be based on this personality profile.

Next, it is time to shop.

This process should be slow and methodical. Don't just run out and buy anything you can get your hands on. You want to make sure the objects speak to you on an intuitive level.

I always recommend that people buy secondhand. It's better for the environment, and thrift stores and antique stores are the best places to find objects from a specific era.

Now, of course you want to be careful about which items you decide to purchase. Keep in mind that you will likely never clear the energy of an object completely. Learn the story of the item as best you can and remember that these sorts of objects could already be anchors for other spirits.

Let's say you purchase an old Scottish flag for your grandpa Jack. You bring it home and hang it above your altar. Before long, you're experiencing a lot of activity, so you assume Grandpa likes the flag. Little do you know, Joe from down the street was extremely attached to that flag, and now he's hanging around your space wondering why you're calling him Grandpa Jack.

For every item you bring into your space, take the time to let its original owner know what you are planning for it and whom you have purchased it for. Not because anything bad will happen, but because it is a courtesy to the previous owner, who may still be attached to it. Chances are everyone involved will be fine with the arrangement.

MAGIC IN THE MUNDANE

Just because you didn't inherit the "valuable stuff" doesn't mean you don't have what you need to create beautiful rituals and spells for your ancestors. This is what I call making magic with the mundane.

The everyday items owned by our loved ones are some of the most overlooked and powerful things you can use in ancestor magic.

Keys, tools, wallets, and cutlery are usually up for grabs when someone's estate is being sorted. While everyone is fighting over Grandma's jewelry box, you can be happy to take the old mixing bowl she used every Sunday to make pancake batter. If someone has claimed your father's collection of baseball cards, ask if you can have his favorite flannel shirt instead.

These are the items that usually contain the most energy because of their importance and the amount they were used by your ancestors.

The following rituals are designed to work with these mundane items. They are accessible and something everyone can do. These talismans and creations may end up being what your own descendants fight over one day because of how special they actually are.

Key charm

Keys are among the most important items we will use in our lifetime. We carry them with us every time we leave the house. We have keys for our front doors, our cars, our offices, and even our mailboxes. I dare you to think of an object you use more than a key. Next to graveyard dirt (pages 75–79) or ashes (page 177), a key is probably the most powerful spirit anchor you can have.

Because keys allow access to something locked or contained, they are often symbolic of gaining knowledge and spiritual wisdom.

Keys also represent being protected from malevolent forces or human foes. Turning a key in a lock can keep whomever we choose from entering a place... or allow someone in. Keys are a symbol of love. One major milestone in most relationships is the act of giving your partner a key. It says you are granting them permission to enter your space whenever they want.

Making a talisman or charm out of a key is a wonderful way to honor the keys left behind by someone who has died.

Directions

Making a key charm is quite simple.

All you need to do is attach a piece of string to the key and hang it on a door, on a window, or at your ancestor altar, or carry it on your person.

However, you can add a bit more magic into the mix by incorporating color, charms, and key types into the charm.

Color

On page 267 you can find a correspondence list for colors and their various meanings.

Key type

Different keys can be used to enhance this charm for different situations.

House key: The home is a place of security, warmth, and love. Only those who are invited in are allowed in. The house key represents family and ancestors. Using a house key for this charm adds a layer of protection to your space.

Office key: Work is where we earn our money, and having a job is a major part of our lives. A charm made from an office or business key can be carried when you need to ask for a raise or promotion, or even to bring a little extra luck into your life when starting your own company.

Car key: A car or other vehicle key symbolizes freedom, travel, and following one's dreams. A car key charm can be kept in your own car or carried on your person for safety and protection while traveling.

Spoon charm

Ask any professional chef or cooking enthusiast what tools they can't live without, and most will answer two things: a sharp knife and a wooden spoon.

Spoons are some of the earliest human tools in existence. They have been around so long that archeologists can't pinpoint exactly where or when they were created, but signs do indicate that the Neanderthals originated the "modern" design of this mini-bowl with a handle (a shell with a long bone attached).

Since then, spoons have been found all over the ancient world, but predominantly in northern Africa, where they were buried alongside mummies in Egypt as grave goods; in China, where they were expertly and ornately crafted from bones and ivory; and in ancient Greece and Rome, where the richest people would be interred with spoons forged in metal.

Wooden spoons took hold in Europe during the medieval and early modern eras. Only the rich could afford fancy silverware. Wood was the material of the people, and that still holds true today.

A good wooden spoon, when properly cared for, can last for around five years before it starts to hold on to bacteria, but most of us keep them a lot longer than that.

If you are in possession of wooden spoons that belonged to your ancestors and have outlived their use, you can repurpose them as charms to hang in your kitchen. They will act as spiritual invitations and talismans for food abundance and prosperity.

What you need

- Wooden spoons
- A woodburning tool
- A pencil
- Hooks or string for hanging

Directions

Lay out your wooden spoons (or other wooden utensils) on a big work space and begin heating up the woodburning tool.

While the woodburner gets warm, take your pencil and draw the sigil of your choice directly on the bowl of the spoon.

Next, carefully trace over your drawing with the woodburner until you have the desired look.

When all your spoons are decorated, you can hang them around your kitchen. Remember that just because a spell or charm seems simple, that doesn't mean it isn't impactful.

> **Pro tip:** If you've never used a woodburner before, I recommend getting one of those heatproof hairstyling gloves to protect yourself from accidental burns.

> **Pro tip:** If you don't have a woodburner, you can use paint instead. Paint also gives you the opportunity to incorporate color into the design.

Shovel healing ritual

Shovels have a long and rich symbolic history. Most people, when asked to think about their cultural or symbolic associations with a shovel, immediately think of groundbreaking. This ritual of moving dirt with a shovel likely evolved from rituals performed across the ancient world when people would build large temples and other places of worship.

For our purposes, shovels represent community development and celebration.

Shovels are also deeply connected to the Underworld and ideas surrounding the afterlife. They shift and turn the ground, which is symbolic of the cycle of life and death. Shovels dig the graves that house our bodies, and shovels cover us with a blanket of earth.

Shovels also symbolize the act of revealing what is hidden below the surface... and for most families, that means secrets and trauma.

As we discussed in chapter 3, "Working with Your Ancestors," a person's journey with ancestral trauma is highly personal and there is no single right way to work through it.

The following ritual is designed to help you either uncover family trauma or begin to put it to rest by using an inherited shovel or spade.

What you need

- An inherited shovel or spade
- Red, pink, and white ribbons
- Paper and a pen
- A small black drawstring bag
- A large plant pot
- Soil
- Mugwort or rosemary seeds (both work well for spiritual communication and protection)
- Optional: sigils

If you did not inherit a shovel, you can buy one! Be sure to cleanse it using the methods on page 170. Once it's cleansed, you can include a surname or family-identifying marker (such as your sigil) when decorating it.

Don't forget to document the process in your BOA!

Directions

The first step of this ritual is to decide whether you want the secrets and trauma out in the open, or if you're ready to put the past to bed for good. Take your time with this step—nothing needs to be decided in an afternoon.

Next comes the creative part: decorating the shovel. If it is made of wood, you may wish to incorporate some of the sigils from the spoon charm and woodburn them onto the staff.

Take your red, pink, and white ribbons and braid them together, then tie the braid to the handle. By braiding pink (self-love and nurturing) and white (healing) with red (bloodline), you are helping to soothe the energy.

Take your piece of paper and write down which family trauma or secret you want to be part of the ritual. Fold the paper three times and place it in your small black bag.

The next steps are done in different ways depending on your goal.

Putting the trauma or secret to rest

Place the black bag in the bottom of the pot and completely fill it with soil.

Bringing the trauma or secret to light

Tie the black bag to the ribbon braid on the handle of the shovel and fill the pot with soil.

After the pot is completely full, stick the shovel into the soil. It's important to have a big enough pot that it can fit the shovel and is sturdy enough to not fall over.

I recommend placing the shovel toward the back edge of the pot so you have more room for the final step.

When everything feels sturdy and secure, sprinkle your mugwort or rosemary seeds into the pot and cover with a thin layer of soil before watering.

As the seeds grow, think about how far you have come in your journey of healing and connecting to your ancestors.

> **TIP:** Rosemary is notoriously hard to sprout from seeds, so if you want, you can buy a small plant from a nursery instead.

More ideas

There are other ways you can incorporate objects into your daily life and your practice. I've listed some in the following pages as a jumping-off point, but don't be afraid to be creative.

HAUNTED HEIRLOOMS

The screaming skull of Burton Agnes Hall

In the charming village of Burton Agnes in Yorkshire, England, there is a beautiful Elizabethan manor called Burton Agnes Hall. This historic house museum and its manicured gardens are open year-round to visitors.

As guests tour the estate, admiring the antique furniture and priceless art, they are often unaware of one special heirloom hidden within the building's walls...a screaming skull.

Though the land has been in the same family since the late 1100s, Burton Agnes Hall was not built until the early seventeenth century, when Sir Henry Griffith moved there with his three daughters.

The girls grew up watching their magnificent home come to fruition, and felt a very strong connection to the hall, particularly the youngest daughter, Anne.

Anne spent her days exploring the rooms and playing in the gardens. She'd regale her family with stories of how she imagined the home would be when it was completed and how she planned to live there forever. Even as she grew into a young woman, she never changed her mind.

One afternoon, Anne went for a walk to the nearby town of Harpham. It was about a mile away and on a route that she had often walked. Unfortunately, on this day, something sinister was lying in wait.

There had been an increase in crime around the countryside, and robbers were lurking on the outskirts of the woods of Burton Agnes Hall.

Anne was robbed and viciously beaten, left for dead by the thugs.

Though she was soon discovered and rushed home, her injuries were serious and the family was told to prepare for her death. For three days the young woman lay in agony, her two sisters at her side.

During this time, Anne made her sisters promise that they would keep a piece of her at the manor forever. She requested that they detach her head from her body and display her skull inside the home.

Though slightly creeped out, her family agreed—likely as a final act of compassion to help soothe their tortured and dying sister.

Relieved that she would remain in the place she loved most for all eternity, Anne finally let go and succumbed to her injuries.

Despite their promise, a few days later Anne's body was interred at the nearby graveyard. Head and all.

The family did their best to move on, but before long strange and terrifying things began to happen in the home.

Night after night, they were awoken by bloodcurdling shrieks, wails, and disembodied voices. At first, they tried to ignore the hauntings, but after a week they couldn't take it.

Anne's coffin was dug up in the hopes that granting her dying wish would end the disturbances...which is exactly what happened.

Her skull was brought into the home, and for a while all was peaceful; until one day, a maid came across the gruesome memento in a cupboard and threw it out the window.

Almost immediately, screams filled the great hall again and continued until the young woman's skull was returned to its rightful spot.

Some years later, the new owners of Burton Agnes Hall attempted to bury Anne's skull in the garden. They felt the stories were just that: stories.

But, as had happened before, Anne's cries of despair echoed through the night.

It was then that the skull was boarded up behind the wood paneling in one of the rooms, never to be removed again.

This unique heirloom will be forever passed along with the estate, and those who know the story can only hope that Anne's spirit remains at peace.

Inheriting a haunted item

While the chances that you will inherit a screaming skull are slim, receiving an heirloom with difficult energy is not out of the realm of possibility.

Working with spirits and ancestors in any form is essentially engaging in a haunting, and there are two types of hauntings that can be attached to an object: intelligent hauntings and residual hauntings.

Working with spirits in the way we do in this book is **intelligent haunting**. It is a conscious and deliberate interaction between ourselves and the spirits.

Using objects as anchors (pages 75–84), we are able to draw our ancestors to us because they contain an energetic imprint from when the person was alive. This imprint is known as a **residual haunting**.

Some objects have a little of this residual energy, while others have a lot, which can manifest in very obvious ways.

In most cases it is the residual energy itself that causes a disturbance. This can be in the form of feelings upon entering a space, sounds, objects moving, and even dreams. At other times, these disturbances are a combination of the residual energy *and* a spirit consciously using that energy to create a disturbance.

The first thing people assume is that the situation is negative or demonic in some way, but that is rarely—if ever—the case. These beliefs are often projections of our own fears in response to the activity.

When dealing with a haunted object, you must ask yourself: Is it negative or am I projecting?

From there, decide: If it isn't negative, then what am I feeling? Confusion? Excitement? Sadness? This part of the process should be approached delicately and with patience. Try not to rush through it.

Because most of the time hauntings occur when you first bring an object into the home, the energy will slowly settle over a few days and the activity will wane. Be sure to give yourself and the energy enough time to get used to each other before moving on to the next steps.

If the energy isn't dissipating or seems to be increasing, there are a few things you can do.

1. Outline your boundaries.

Make your personal and home rules known to the spirit. If they cannot respect them, then they will have to leave. You may find it helpful to recite your list of boundaries from chapter 3!

Think about what you would expect of a living person in this situation. Would you allow them to run around your home completely unchecked and misbehaving? Probably not.

Everyone has a different threshold of activity they are willing to allow. Work with the spirits to figure out what is right for you both.

2. Try dampening or suppressing the energy.

Sometimes if setting boundaries isn't working well or is taking too long to kick in, you can use other items to counteract the energy and keep it under control.

The first way to do this is by gently cleansing the item with smoke from plants or resins. Cleansing items is tricky, because you don't want to get rid of the spiritual energy completely, you just want to calm it down.

Opt for herbs like chamomile, lavender, and lemon balm, which are more for soothing than banishing.

Burn the herbs and pass the item through the smoke (for furniture, you can move the smoke around the piece).

Pros: Easily accessible, can be repeated as often as needed, and is typically effective.

Cons: May work too well, and smoke can damage items, leaving a smell or discoloration.

The second option for dampening energy is to try some grounding. This is done using gemstones or crystals.

Place one or two next to or on top of the object when it is not in use to help ground or even absorb the energy.

My personal recommendation would be to use black tourmaline or pink Himalayan salt. Both are believed to release negative ions and shift the energy of an environment.

Pros: Easily accessible, and the gemstones or crystals work around the clock.

Cons: The mining industry for crystals can be extremely exploitative, and some crystals can be expensive. Make sure you source your crystals responsibly.

3. Remove the object.

Sometimes, despite your best intentions, an object just needs to be removed from the home. If your boundaries, cleansing, and subduing don't work, you may need to part ways. As we learned from Burton Agnes Hall, this can have its own consequences, but thankfully that sort of haunting is rare.

If you can't bear to get rid of the object altogether, try switching its location or putting it into storage for a while.

AT REST

CHAPTER EIGHT

BURIALS AND FUNERAL CUSTOMS

8

Burials and Funeral Customs

RESTING PLACES

There are two main types of resting places that you will come across in your work with your ancestors: traditional burial and cremation.

Whatever place our body goes after death becomes our grave. Some graves are permanent and fixed in one location, such as in a plot in a cemetery, while other graves, such as a cinerary urn, can move around or even be passed down through the family every few decades.

Each grave is as unique as the person who occupies it. Some graves lie in wait for centuries, hoping to be discovered and honored once more, while others are continuously overflowing with offerings and other trinkets for decades at a time.

Burial

As traditional in-ground burials have been the most popular for the last few centuries, they are likely the type you will come across most in your research about your ancestors.

We explore cemeteries and headstones in depth in chapter 9.

Many animals mourn and even ritualize the dead, but the acts of burying the dead and deliberately revisiting those remains are very human.

For humans, burying the dead has both practical and spiritual implications.

Burials take place in holes dug into the ground, inside special buildings, or in structures known as tombs.

The reason for this is that bodies decay. This not only poses a health risk for the living, it can also be disturbing to see someone we once loved begin to decompose.

(While some cultures do work with the mummified or skeletal remains of their ancestors, that is a very different situation and requires specific conditions and processes. The early stages of decomposition are not part of the scenario.)

Not only does burial protect us from grisly sights, but it also keeps wild animals from damaging or stealing parts of the body. Many religions believe that the body is needed in the afterlife and so should be kept intact.

History of burial

Archeologists believe that the first hominid species to intentionally bury their dead were the Neanderthals. In 1908 a Neanderthal grave was discovered in a cave in France, containing stone tools alongside the deceased Neanderthal man's skeleton, tools his community clearly believed he would need in the afterlife.

DID YOU KNOW?

Humans and Neanderthals began interbreeding about sixty-five thousand years ago, and many of us alive today still carry approximately 1 to 3 percent of Neanderthal DNA.

When it comes to *Homo sapiens*, we have also been burying the dead for basically just as long as the Neanderthals, and this took place congruently around the world.

The Sumerians of ancient Mesopotamia gifted us with a lot of disciplines and inventions we still enjoy today. Agriculture, astrology, writing, and even spoked wheels come to us thanks to this group of people, who lived from 8000 to 2000 BCE.

The Sumerians believed that all people ended up in the Underworld. This was a dark place under the ground that was something of a shadow version of the living world.

To ensure a swift journey to this land, people were interred below the ground.

Most people were buried underneath the family home so that their graves were easily accessible for maintenance and ritual purposes. Because the only food and water the dead could receive in the Underworld came from offerings left by the living, accessibility was incredibly important.

Though the ancient Greeks who lived in Athens preferred cremation, many other ancient Greeks opted for burials instead.

They believed that an unburied body was an affront to the gods, so the burial process was an important part of life.

For many centuries, in-ground graves would house multiple bodies as well as plenty of offerings to accompany the spirits into the afterlife. Around 1100 BCE, the Greeks began assigning people their own individual graves. It was also during this time that grave goods became less common.

The Maya practiced both burial and cremation. Graves ranged from simple single-person plots to elaborate tombs outfitted for kings and queens.

The average Mayan person was buried under the floor of their home, at their place of work, or next to a temple or other religious site.

As the Maya's religious systems evolved over the centuries, so did the position in which they laid the dead. Archeologists say they can never be certain of which direction and position the person will be placed in until they see it.

Casket vs. coffin

Deciding what you will be buried in is as important a decision as where you want to be buried. These days, the choice is often left up to loved ones of the deceased, but it wasn't always that way.

Not too long ago, it was common for people to both build and store their own coffins in their homes. They knew death could strike at any time and they wanted to make sure things were ready.

DID YOU KNOW?

There is a difference between a casket and a coffin.

A **casket** is a four-sided rectangular body box with a hinged lid. The name comes

from the French word *cassette*, which means a box to house precious goods.

Caskets come in two main styles, known as a full couch and a half couch. The full couch means the entire lid lifts as one piece when opened. The half couch means the lid opens in two parts independently of each other.

These days caskets are often highly decorative, with carved designs and metal hardware as accents. One of these accents is what is known as a casket plate. These little metal rectangles are engraved with words or phrases such as "Our Darling" or "Father." Before the casket is buried, the plate will sometimes be removed and kept as a memento.

Caskets came into fashion sometime in the late nineteenth century in the USA and Canada; before that time, these two countries had not yet established a woodworking industry that could meet the growing demand of death. Because the new caskets had only four sides, they could be produced at a faster rate than the usually six-sided coffins that had preceded them.

A **coffin** is a six-sided or hexagonal box that begins narrow at the top where the head would be, widens at the shoulders, and then tapers in again along the legs and toward the feet.

Coffins are generally lightly lined with a simple fabric and are not too over-the-top in terms of embellishments, though some can be quite decorative. In terms of materials, they are generally less expensive, but a coffin can sometimes cost more if they are not widely used in your region and have to be imported or custom-made.

It's important to note that in some countries, such as the UK, the word "coffin" is used to mean both caskets and coffins.

Cremation

Cremation is the process of burning a body in a special chamber or oven that can heat up to 1,800 degrees Fahrenheit. During this process, almost all the carbon in the body is removed and what is left is calcium phosphate (bone fragments) and a few other minerals.

From there, the fragments are ground up into a powder (known as cremains or ashes) and placed in a cinerary urn.

History of cremation

On July 15, 1968, in the now-dried-up Lake Mungo in Australia, a young geologist came across bone fragments embedded in the wall of his dig.

Mungo Lady, as she was affectionately named, is the oldest surviving evidence of a cremation process anywhere in the world.

At forty thousand years old, she is also believed by some to be the oldest evidence of a ceremonial burial, or funeral if you will.

When she was excavated, archeologists determined that she had been burned, and then her bones had been crushed and burned again before being decorated with red ochre and carefully buried.

By 2500 to 1000 BCE, the practice of cremation had spread to Europe and was being used in the British Isles, Portugal, Spain, Hungary, Italy, and Greece.

The Greek poet and philosopher Homer wrote extensively about cremation, and the Romans too adopted the process in 600 BCE.

The Romans preferred to cremate the dead by placing the body on pine logs filled with resins, which would release a sweet-smelling aroma to help mask the scent of burning flesh. Afterward, all bone fragments would be collected and placed in a special cinerary urn.

For the Vikings, cremation was a massive affair. Food, jewelry, and other offerings would be added to the pyre with the body. Unfortunately, that wasn't all that would be sacrificed for the deceased. Sometimes a woman or women would be killed and burned to act as companions for a deceased man. However, if it was a woman who had died, no men were burned in her honor...how curious.

In 400 CE, as Christianity became the dominant religion of Europe, cremation fell out of favor.

Occasionally, exceptions would be made for cremation, such as situations relating to mass death like wars and plagues, but other than that it wasn't common.

Of course, whatever body disposal methods were popular in England spread to the rest of the British Empire. Basically, wherever the English colonized, burial practices went with them.

In the late nineteenth century, cremation came back into fashion due to the rapid growth of the population in Europe and North America.

These days cremation is the fastest-growing method of body disposal because of the lack of space and the rising costs of burials.

Though Europe went through many periods of not using cremation, it has remained the top choice in many other cultures and religions. For Buddhists and Hindus, cremation is a mandatory part of their faiths.

FUNERALS

My first funeral

The first funeral I can remember was for my maternal grandfather. It was an open-casket funeral and the first time I had seen him since the day he died—an event that marked my initial foray into the realm of the spirits.

Through all the condolences and heartfelt sentiments, I could still hear on the floor of the funeral parlor the shuffle of the moccasin-style slippers he always wore around the house—a sound that would have been impossible for anyone to replicate, since the chapel room was mostly carpeted. I wondered if (and hoped) he was walking around listening to all the stories being shared about him. He was the type who would've loved to attend his own funeral: checking out who was there and chiming in with little jokes or anecdotes about his life.

He would've especially liked to watch my little cousin Alexandra go around and announce to the guests that "Dzedo is sleeping in the basket," her adorable mispronunciation of the word "casket."

She was too young to understand the finality of death, and I envied her. To Alexandra, our grandfather was just asleep; later he would wake up, and they would play a game or read a story together.

Though she couldn't quite grasp what was happening, she did understand the importance of the situation. She knew it was a special day and that there were many people she needed to inform about the "basket."

We can learn something valuable from my cousin Alexandra about how we might approach ancestor work, and that is this: there is nothing to fear about honoring the death of our loved ones. The fear around death comes from the torture of learning that we are all mortal—something Alexandra hadn't been burdened with yet.

All she knew was that everyone she loved was there and that all would be fine; her dzedo was safe, asleep in the basket.

History of funeral homes

The idea of a professional establishment where people could have help preparing the dead for burial became popular in the 1860s in the United States.

Before then, the body would be tended to by the family of the deceased in their own home (or the home of a close relative), where the funeral would also take place.

All the washing and dressing of the body was done by the family, while neighbors and friends pitched in where they could by either building a coffin or helping out with chores.

The existence of the modern funeral home is in part thanks to the assassination of Abraham Lincoln. He was America's favorite president, and his death shook its people to the core. It was decided that he would have a large funeral procession lasting several weeks, and so he was embalmed to prevent decay.

Because he was so adored, when people found out he was embalmed they wanted the same treatment for their loved ones. Because of the sudden demand for this procedure, specialized facilities began to spring up overnight.

Death and capitalism officially hit it off.

Other benefits of funeral homes quickly began to reveal themselves. Because bodies could now stay fresh longer, the funerals themselves could be pushed back a few days to allow family members and friends who weren't nearby to travel.

Funeral homes also took over the majority of funeral arrangements and preparation, which gave the family more time to get their affairs in order and to grieve.

The term "undertaker" was born out of this concept: the person in charge literally "undertook" the responsibility of the funeral arrangements and body care.

Types of funerals

There is no one right way to have a funeral. Procedures and customs are informed by various factors such as religion, personal taste, and budget.

Most funerals follow a "traditional" setup, which is specific to the deceased's culture and religion. Below is just a sample of how different cultures and communities honor their dead.

Western funerals

In the West, most funerals tend to follow a specific pattern or chain of events that contains the remnants of Christian customs blended with modern ideas surrounding death. Despite some lingering religious associations, funerals can be quite secular, unless of course the deceased is a practicing member of a faith.

First, the body is taken to a funeral home, which is where it will be prepared for the funeral.

At the home, it is embalmed (a special process in which the blood is replaced with a chemical to keep the body from decomposing). Then the person is dressed and placed in a special refrigerator for preservation.

Next, there is the visitation or wake. A visitation is an informal gathering or ceremony where friends and family can come to pay their respects to the dead at their convenience at one or two set times. The visitation is generally the day or evening before the formal funeral.

Following the visitation is the funeral. This can be held in the funeral home, at a place of worship, or at the site at which the body will be interred.

The agenda for a funeral is called the order of service, and while funerals can vary, they do tend to contain a few elements from the following list:

- Opening words (sometimes scripture)
- Eulogy (a speech of remembrance—see chapter 6)
- Tributes from family
- Tributes from friends
- Poem or scripture
- Closing words

After the funeral comes the reception. A reception is very similar to a visitation in that it is an informal gathering to honor the deceased, but it typically takes place after the funeral in someone's home or a restaurant, and the body is not present.

Traditional Jewish funeral

When a Jewish person dies, they are buried as quickly as possible; there is almost no time between the death and the interment of their body.

Upon death, the first step is contacting the synagogue or rabbi of the congregation the person belongs to. The synagogue will take over the arrangements (unless the deceased had special requests) and begin the preparations for burial.

First, the body is washed completely, and during this process, it is forbidden for it to be placed facedown. Someone is always with the body in order to protect it both physically and spiritually.

Jewish people are never embalmed, though the practice is growing increasingly popular among the secular population. The body is then placed in a simple pine casket.

In terms of the actual funeral, it is often very simple and short: a eulogy is read, along with psalms and a special blessing for the deceased.

Sometimes black ribbons are handed out to the family; at other times, family members make a small tear in their clothes to symbolize their loss.

After the body has been interred, the family will sit shiva, a period of mourning in which family members stay in the house and accept condolences and visitors. Traditionally this lasts seven days, but these days shiva often goes on for about three. During shiva, mirrors are covered, and it is important that the family not worry about mundane or trivial matters.

Traditional Hindu funeral

In the Hindu faith, it is believed that the soul of a person is indestructible and will be reincarnated until it reaches moksha, which means it has found its perfect form. Once the soul reaches this state, rebirth is no longer necessary and it becomes one with the divine.

When a person of Hindu faith dies, it is believed that the body has served its purpose, and therefore it is cremated, usually within twenty-four hours; because this process is quick, embalming of the body is unnecessary.

During the time between death and cremation, the body stays at home, where it is washed and anointed with essential oils.

The body is then placed in an open casket, and all guests are invited to view it and pay their respects; however, it is important that the body is not touched, as this is seen as disrespectful. During the funeral, prayers and mantras are recited, led by a priest or a high-ranking male of the family.

After the funeral, the deceased is transported to the cremation site. Histor-

O'SULLIVAN URNS

Manufacturing in quantity always lowers cost. We make monuments in large and therefore can sell monuments of equal quality for a lower price the small dealer who makes only a few stones a month.

1010, 1015, 1020, 1025, 1030, 1035, 1038,
1045, 1050, 1055

ically this was done at the Ganges River, but nowadays the process is handled locally (which is helpful for people living far away).

The day after the funeral, the cremains are scattered at a river or a significant location for the deceased.

The next thirty days or so are spent in mourning by the family. Photos are displayed and decorated with flower garlands.

After the thirteenth day of mourning, the family performs a ritual to release the soul of the deceased so they may be reincarnated.

Traditional Chinese funeral

Ancestor veneration is a major part of Chinese culture, as you learned from the naming customs in chapter 5, so it is no surprise that the Chinese traditionally hold grand funerals for their loved ones.

When a Chinese person dies, the first step is typically to contact a fêng shui master to help choose the appropriate time for the funeral as well as the correct grave site.

The visitation prior to the funeral typically lasts around three days, during which time family and friends can come to pay their respects.

Unlike here in the West, where black is the assigned color for matters relating to death, white is the color of mourning in China. The deceased is dressed in a special white burial robe. Sometimes, if a person lived beyond the age of eighty, they can be dressed in bright colors, like red.

After the visitation period has passed, the casket is closed. It is important for the members of the family to have their backs toward the casket as it is closed in order to prevent their souls from being trapped inside.

During the funeral, the family members will burn special paper known as joss paper. Joss paper is a type of spirit money that ensures that the needs of the deceased will be met in the afterlife.

Guests of the funeral are required to offer a donation of money to the family of the deceased, with $101 being the customary amount.

Other times, red threads are gifted to the family by guests. These are then tied to doors in order to protect the family from evil spirits during this vulnerable time.

CHAPTER NINE

A GUIDE TO CEMETERIES

9

A Guide to Cemeteries

A GRAVE MATTER

In order to work effectively with your ancestors, you need to embrace the state they are in: death. There is nowhere more appropriate for this than a cemetery or graveyard.

Inside the cemetery there is an entire world full of rich symbolism, stories, and, of course, spirits.

For many people, thinking about death and cemeteries can conjure up a wide range of emotions, many of which are contradictory.

For those of us who were born in the last seventy years, our relationship with death looks different than it did for our parents and grandparents. There is a degree of separation between ourselves and death. While in some circumstances that can be seen as a positive—such as not having to kill our own livestock—it can also be a negative, as it gives us the ability to tune out death when it makes us uncomfortable.

However we feel about death, when it appears in our life in the form of losing a loved one, it is painful. Not only are we in pain over our loss, but we are also forced to think about our own mortality.

The cemetery has a practical and a spiritual purpose, both of which you will learn in this chapter. If your culture doesn't use a cemetery as a final resting place, you can still utilize this chapter to work with community or vocational ancestors, as well as the plants and animals that inhabit the area.

I have been a tombstone tourist—which is a fancy term for someone who likes cemeteries—since I was a little girl. This is a trait I inherited from my maternal grandfather. Not only did he love the history that is found in cemeteries, but he was also involved in restoration projects in graveyards and cemeteries outside Toronto.

My grandfather instilled in me the importance of having a final resting place, and really impressed upon me just how much power a gravestone holds.

In 1976, a good twelve years before I was born, tragedy struck when my grandparents' dog, Buffy, was poisoned by a neighbor and killed. It was a cruel fate for any pet to experience, and my grandfather felt she deserved more. She deserved a proper burial.

In the woods behind their house there is a small hill, reminiscent of an ancient tumulus or passage tomb, and inside this hill rests Buffy. On top of her grave, surrounded by birch and maple trees, there is a rock with an epitaph crudely carved into its surface by my uncle, who was very bonded to her: BUFFY 1976.

I never met Buffy while she was alive, but we did get to know each other quite well throughout my life. Buffy's headstone is where I did all my best thinking as a child. I'd tell her all my hopes and dreams. She was home base for hide-and-seek. She was the keeper of many tears after my grandfather died—a story I told in *The Book of Séances*.

Despite my having inherited my love of cemetery history and storytelling from both my maternal grandparents, there have been many times when I have felt like an outsider around that side of the family.

Being an introvert in a room full of extroverts can be overwhelming and surprisingly lonely.

I have always been compared to my dad and his side of the family because of this. I look and act a lot like him. I inherited his green eyes, shy disposition, and sarcastic sense of humor.

One thing I don't have in common with my dad is that I love talking about my ancestors, whereas he has the tendency to be tight-lipped about his family line. Addiction trauma has plagued my paternal ancestry for over a century, trauma that has also become part of my identity. I know that this can make opening up difficult.

So when I discovered that most of my paternal ancestors who moved to Canada in the late 1800s were buried in a cemetery just twenty minutes from my home, it became a place of refuge and discovery.

The first time I stood among these gravestones, I felt understood, like an entire new world had opened up to me.

Suddenly there was a place I could go to get to know the people I inherited all these qualities from—qualities that had once made me feel left out.

I visit these ancestors often. I tend to their graves, and I tell them about my life. I match the faces in the very few photographs I have to the names carved in the stones.

I share stories with them about how the world has changed, and they share stories with me: either by way of my research, using the information provided by their gravestones, or by my using methods of divination, such as my oracle cards. In one instance, my cards directed me to the hidden location of a family headstone—another story that I recount in *The Book of Séances*.

Once I had spent a good amount of time at the cemetery, I started sharing my discoveries with my dad...and a funny thing happened: he started sharing back.

Soon, he began volunteering information: facts he thinks might be helpful or theories that fill in gaps. He's even said he will help me get custody of our ancestors' cemetery plots, whose ownership was never transferred upon each death. This complicated process speaks to the importance of crafting your own death plan—see chapter 10.

The magic of the cemetery isn't just about casting spells or looking for ghosts; it can also be about transforming the relationship you have with your family and the way you feel about yourself.

In the cemetery, family comes together: alive and dead.

BOA EXERCISE

The first exercise to try in the cemetery section of your BOA is a simple one.

Tell the story of your first cemetery experience, or one that has special significance for you.

It's okay if you can't remember all the details perfectly; what matters is that you are sharing something intimate with your ancestors and your descendants.

The following prompts can help you get started:

- What is the name of the cemetery?
- Do you know its history?
- Are relatives buried there?
- How old were you when you visited?
- What do you remember most?
- Did you visit with family members?
- Did you understand what a cemetery was?
- Did you have a favorite headstone?
- Have you been back since?

HISTORY AND TERMINOLOGY

Though used interchangeably today, the terms **graveyard**, **churchyard**, and **cemetery** all have slightly different meanings.

A **graveyard** is a plot of land designated for burying the dead. Graveyards are usually rural and attached to a specific religion.

A **churchyard** is the land attached to a church, which *can* contain a graveyard but doesn't always. In Scotland, a churchyard is known as a **kirkyard**.

A **cemetery** is a plot of land designated for burying the dead that is either government-run or privately owned, and is open to everyone regardless of ethnicity, gender, or faith.

Throughout this book I use the term "cemetery," but most of the hands-on information can be applied to graveyards and other burial grounds as well.

HOW DID THE CEMETERY COME TO BE?

In the 1700s and 1800s, Europe began to see an explosion in population due to advancements in medicine and industry. Before 1750, people had a life expectancy of only thirty-five. Many children would never see adulthood or have children of their own. As people began to live longer, more of those children grew up and started their own families. Cities and towns began to expand rapidly, and the local church graveyards could not keep up with the burial demand.

Before this growth, many poor people could not afford their own burial plots, which were reserved for the rich or well-known people in society. Most often the poor would be placed in large mass graves; they would sometimes receive a gravestone or marker, but this was rare.

But now people were beginning to see an increase in wages. While there was still a massive divide between the haves and the have-nots, the "middle class" as we know it today was beginning to form. More and more people wanted a grave plot for themselves and their family. A person's having "made it" wasn't reflected in the shoes they wore, it was seen in what graveyard section they had secured and what their gravestone looked like.

In 1804 the Père Lachaise Cemetery opened in Paris. It was a city-run garden cemetery and the first of its kind in France.

The architect Alexandre-Théodore Brongniart had been tasked with designing the grounds. Inspired by British gardens and architecture, Brongniart included beautiful winding paths and roads throughout the acres. The cemetery was then filled with trees and other greenery.

When the cemetery opened its gates for burials, the response was underwhelming. Many religious people were uneasy with being buried somewhere other than a graveyard.

In order to increase popularity, Père Lachaise's operators moved famous French citizens such as Molière from their current resting places to Père Lachaise. The marketing scheme was a great success, and by the 1830s, more than thirty thousand burials had taken place there.

Meanwhile, the British public was growing tired of the church's involvement in every aspect of life and took notice of these new garden cemeteries.

In the 1830s, the British government began legislating and building non-denominational cemeteries on the edges of cities and towns.

As more and more people moved to the USA and the colonies that now make up Canada, the garden cemetery came with them.

In both of these countries, many garden cemeteries are inside the city limits and were actually the first urban public parks and recreational areas.

In Toronto, where I live, it's quite normal to go visit and spend time in the major cemeteries. Every day people walk their dogs, jog, bike, and even eat lunch in them. I myself can be found there at least once or twice a week in the warmer months.

While religious graveyards continued to thrive during the rise of the garden cemetery and other state-run cemeteries, they have become less popular each year in urban settings.

Today, there are a wide variety of cemeteries in the USA and Canada, including religious cemeteries, urban cemeteries, private family cemeteries, and military cemeteries, as well as Black and enslaved people's cemeteries and Indigenous burial grounds.

If you are not Indigenous, please respect that these burial areas are not open to non-Indigenous people—even to visit. If you are curious about the land and territory you occupy, please seek out an Indigenous-run cultural center or organization.

Some enslaved people's cemeteries are also closed to visitors because of their archeological significance, as well as their spiritual significance.

You can find a list of cemetery- and burial-related resources at the back of this book.

WHAT CAN BE FOUND IN A CEMETERY?

Understanding what you see at a cemetery is important for your spiritual and ancestral work.

The boundaries of a cemetery are usually determined by a gate or a wall. The entrance is known as the **lych-gate**. Traditionally the lych-gate had a wooden roof and was used to protect the casket while the funeral party arrived at the cemetery, but now the term encompasses all entrances.

When you cross through this gate, understand that you are entering the realm of the dead.

You may notice that there are sections that seem to be populated by only one ethnicity or religion.

There are two reasons for this:

The first is that for a long time, segregation was not only socially acceptable, but also written into the law. Against their original, inclusive designs, some cemeteries did not permit the burial of Black folks, as recently as fifty years ago. Others would relegate Catholics to a specific section and Protestants to another.

Thankfully, today nobody can be prevented from purchasing a plot based on ethnicity or faith.

The second reason a cemetery may be divided by ethnicity is if the neighborhood surrounding it is populated by a specific community. For instance, you may notice large sections of stones containing only—say—Polish names; this is simply because people tend to buy plots near their already-interred family.

I recommend copying the following list into your BOA. Depending on your location, the terminology may vary slightly.

Grave: A place where a body or the cremains of a deceased person are laid to rest. This is usually a hole dug in a cemetery or graveyard that is marked with a monument, but can also be a spot in a tomb, a sepulcher, or a mausoleum.

Plot: A designated area in a cemetery where a grave can be dug; plots are the unit of measurement people purchase for the grave. They are often categorized into "single" and "double" options.

Gravestone: A stone that marks the spot of a grave and identifies its occupant.

Headstone: A large gravestone that is placed at the "head" of a grave. Can be used with a footstone or on its own. Headstones come in a variety of shapes and styles; the most common is a vertical style. Headstones have a base that is either above the surface or hidden below it. The base is what keeps them upright.

Footstone: Used in conjunction with a headstone, this small grave marker is placed at the "foot" of a grave. This stone will generally only include the initials of the name inscribed on the headstone. Sometimes these stones can be used alone, but only when part of a larger family plot. In this instance they will either have initials or a single word, such as "Daughter" or "Father."

Tombstone: Another word for a gravestone, or a gravestone used inside a tomb.

(It is acceptable to use "gravestone," "headstone," and "tombstone" interchangeably, so feel free to pick a term that feels right for you. I personally prefer the terms "gravestone" and "headstone.")

Family stone: A gravestone that marks a family plot and not an individual grave.

Ledger stone: A gravestone that is rectangular in shape, lies flat on the ground, and is flush with the surface of the earth. In some places the term "ledger stone" is used to describe a rectangular stone that may or may not be flush with the earth and covers the entire length of the body.

Bevel marker: A gravestone that is in the shape of a wedge of cheese. The back of the gravestone is higher than the front. These can also be called slant markers.

Grave house: A houselike structure built around a grave that is most commonly found in the American South and constructed of wood.

Cairn: A structure made of rocks that are piled on top of a grave.

Sepulcher: An area used for burial that is typically cut into a rock formation.

Cenotaph: A memorial or marker for a grave that does not contain a body. Usually these are erected to commemorate someone who was lost at sea or went missing in a war.

Grave fence: A fence that outlines a grave plot in its entirety.

Tomb: A burial chamber. Historically, tombs have been underground, in caves, or inside a man-made area, like a chamber dug into the side of a hill.

Mausoleum: A freestanding structure that houses the remains of the deceased.

ANATOMY OF A GRAVESTONE

In addition to their physical style and design characteristics, grave markers include a number of content components as well.

The first and arguably most important part of a gravestone is the **epitaph**.

An epitaph is an inscription that contains biographical information about the grave's occupant, such as name, birth date, death date, family role (mother, father, etc.), profession, and religious affiliation.

Epitaphs can also include poems, mourning phrases, and funny anecdotes describing the deceased. Some epitaphs state the cause of death. My third great-grandfather Charles's obelisk headstone reads:

> In Memory
> *Charles Goodchild*
> **Killed by Accident**
> **At Murray Hill**
> **November 15th 1898**
> **Aged 63 Years**

The Murray Hill disaster was a preventable train crash that took the lives of twelve people near Trenton, Ontario, in 1898. The Grand Trunk Railway quickly removed all mention of Murray Hill on their maps after the disaster, and the local community seems to have renamed the area as well. The exact location is still unknown, but I have investigated three possibilities.

Symbols and decorations play an important role in the gravestone message as well. Each engraving you come across has a deliberate meaning that can provide insight into your ancestors. I have compiled a dictionary of the most popular symbols beginning on page 227.

Having a basic knowledge of the **material** a gravestone is made of is important not only for the care and upkeep of the stone, but for magical purposes as well. In witchcraft, rocks and minerals have their own spiritual and metaphysical associations, and this is extended to items crafted with them.

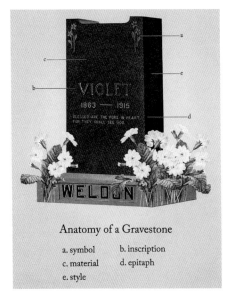

Anatomy of a Gravestone

a. symbol   b. inscription
c. material   d. epitaph
e. style

For eons, many grave markers were carved from **wood** due to cost or limited resources. Unfortunately, wood rots and deteriorates, so such markers are rarely found these days. If you do come across an old wood marker, chances are it was crafted from a local tree and may be identifiable. If so, be sure to check out the "Flora: plants of the dead" list later in this chapter.

Granite: 1920 to present

For a hundred years or so now, granite has been the top choice for gravestones. It not only polishes beautifully, but it also comes in a variety of colors and patterns and withstands a wide range of temperatures and weather patterns.

The main metaphysical and magical properties associated with granite are grounding and protection, but many people also claim that this rock is great for communication and divination.

Marble: 1800 to 1930

Marble is a metamorphic rock that was a very popular choice for headstones and other cemetery architecture at one time due to its beauty and intricate patterns.

Unfortunately, American marble is quite soft and deteriorates if left vulnerable to the elements. Inscriptions in marble can become illegible over time.

In a magical sense, marble is believed to be calming and nurturing. Some marbles contain high amounts of calcite, which is thought to be cleansing of negative energy.

Slate: 1650 to 1800

Slate is another metamorphic rock formerly used for gravestones and was the material of choice in early Colonial America. The puritan graveyards of New England are full of these dark-gray stones.

Unlike marble, slate holds up extremely well to temperature and weather changes and is exceptional for showcasing details and other intricate designs. Many of the headstones from the mid-1700s still look to be in perfect condition.

As you learned in chapter 4, slate is an important material for ancestor work. A slate headstone fosters family and community bonding and aids in protection and grounding.

Soapstone: 1750 to 1950

Soapstone is a metamorphic rock that is comprised of mostly talc and iron. You can test whether a gravestone is indeed soapstone by touching it with a small magnet and seeing if the magnet sticks.

Soapstone was a good choice for gravestones because it is easy to carve.

Its metaphysical and magical associations are familial bonding and trauma healing, due to the iron content. Two-thirds of the iron content found in the human body is in our red blood cells.

Limestone: 1650 to 1900

Because limestone is a sedimentary rock and more vulnerable to water and chemicals, it isn't a good choice for gravestones. However, historically it was a popular choice in many cemeteries and graveyards. Limestone is easily obtained from many different locations and is easy to carve.

Lichen is especially attracted to limestone, and removing it is difficult because it can erode the rock or take pieces of the stone with it. Without upkeep and professional care, limestone monuments often fall into disrepair.

One unique quality of limestone is that it can contain fossils. Your gravestone may be the resting place for ancient animal and plant spirits.

The magical properties of limestone are grounding, protection, and healing.

White bronze: 1870 to 1930

Metal typically only appears in cemeteries as an accent on monuments, but in the mid- to late 1800s, the Monumental Bronze Company of Bridgeport, Connecticut, created an alloy of copper, tin, and zinc that had a bluish-white color they called white bronze, which was used in a smattering of gravestones.

This new material was resistant to lichen and cheaper than granite and could be formed into many different elaborate designs.

THE ARCHER HEADSTONE COMPANY

work is personally inspected and guaranteed to be first-class

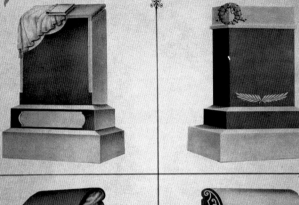

684

Slab 6.6x3.0x0.6
Die 2.4x1.2x2.0
    Height, 2.6; Weight, 2880 lbs.
    Ga. Marble . . $225.00
    Italian . . . 250.00
    If carving on corners of die is
not desired, deduct $30.00.

Magically, zinc is excellent for dispelling negativity and enhancing communication. Tin is great for broadening our horizons and opinions and increasing our luck. And copper is hands down one of the best materials for spirit communication and divination.

Other materials and markers

Income played a large role in what gravestones people could afford over the last few centuries. Many plots would have simple rocks known as fieldstones placed on them as temporary markers. The family would leave them there in the hopes that one day they could afford a fancier gravestone for their loved one.

In early Black cemeteries, markers can sometimes be hard to recognize. Because few to no resources were available for enslaved people, graves were marked with rocks, fieldstones, shells, and tree stumps. In some instances, Black mourners were allowed to craft wooden markers, but there was always the threat that they would be desecrated. Using discreet markers allowed family members to pay tribute to their loved ones as well as mourn them with less fear, though it was an unwanted necessity.

Activity: Design a mini-gravestone

For those of us who use gravestones to mark burial places, this can be a wonderful activity to try.

If your ancestors don't use gravestones, you are welcome to skip this activity or adjust it to suit your needs. Not all memorial monuments need to be traditional gravestones, either. Plaques, garden rocks, or small signs are great alternatives. Get creative with it.

Gravestones and other monuments say to the world, "I existed." They mark a sacred spot in the land. They are important for both the dead and the living because they are something we can see, touch, and focus on.

The following activity can be very meaningful for your ancestors who were not able or allowed to have a gravestone of their own.

My reason for creating this activity is to honor my paternal grandfather, Charlie, who passed away in 1992, when I was four years old. Even though all his family members and ancestors (of those who immigrated to Canada) are buried in the same cemetery, burial was not something my grandmother could afford for him, so he was cremated. Though interring cremains was an option, it was still out of her price range.

My grandmother is believed to have spread Charlie's cremains sometime before her death in 1998, but if she told anyone where that was, they have long since forgotten and nobody felt the need to write this information down.

I know that if money hadn't been a factor, my grandfather would have preferred to be buried in the cemetery alongside his parents.

By participating in this gravestone exercise, I am not only performing an act of love and respect, but I am also building an additional anchor point for his spirit.

What you need

- Your BOA
- Pencils, crayons, or other art supplies
- Optional: clay and paint, mini-gravestone models

Steps

Begin by deciding which of your ancestors needs (or wants) a gravestone.

I would only perform this ritual after conducting extensive research about the location of your ancestor's burial or cremains, as your ancestor may already have a monument.

The next step is to dedicate a page of your BOA to this ancestor. Use the ritual ink we made on page 25 to write their name at the top of the page, and the following dedication statement. Feel free to modify it to suit your needs.

I [Your Name] dedicate this monument in honor of [Ancestor's Name], for [they did not have a gravestone of their own/their gravestone was destroyed/ their gravestone could not be located].

Mine looks like this:

I, Claire Goodchild, dedicate this gravestone design to Charles William Goodchild, for he did not have a gravestone of his own.

Next comes the fun part, designing the monument!

Unlike designing a burial gravestone, money is no object in this exercise. Try to consider your ancestor's wants and personal taste as you brainstorm ideas for their gravestone. If they were shy or modest, a simple stone may be fitting. For the flashy types (like my grandfather), an ornately carved monument may be more their taste.

Include some of the symbols in the dictionary section beginning on page 227 to add some extra power to the design.

Use the following template to record your choices:

Gravestone type:

Material:

Symbols and meanings:

Epitaph:

After you've decided on and recorded your choices, it's time to get out your art supplies and draw the gravestone.

I want to stress that this activity can be done by anyone regardless of artistic ability. What matters to your ancestor is the intent.

As you create this artwork, you may find it helpful to imagine what sorts of offerings you would leave for your ancestor if this gravestone existed in the real world.

(Be mindful of your surroundings while you do this exercise. Your ancestor may join you in the space. I would encourage you to speak out loud to them.)

Now, you can either finish the activity here, or take it one step further by making clay model gravestones for your ancestor altar.

This can be the gravestone you just designed, or you may want to make mini-replicas of existing stones. These models can be a nice addition to your altar space if you live far away from the cemetery.

Additional ideas

You may want to mix grave dirt or dried herbs in with the clay to enhance the gravestones further.

If model making is not your thing, many hobby and gaming stores sell premade miniature headstone models that can be decorated. Halloween is a great time to stock up!

Caring for gravestones

Caring for your ancestors' gravestones and other memorials is an important part of your ancestor practice and spirit work.

In order not to harm or damage a gravestone, there are a few tips you should keep in mind.

Small actions like gently brushing off debris are typically safe, but don't tug at roots or vines that have attached themselves in cracks or crevices of the gravestone.

If a stone is crumbling or brittle in any way, leave it be.

Never use metal scrapers or stiff bristle brushes on a gravestone.

Most cemeteries will do maintenance for a fee, but many caretakers will help you out for free if they recognize you. Other than the cemetery guardian, these people are your best allies.

If someone who works for the cemetery tells you not to do something because it is harmful, trust that they know best.

And finally, understand that older gravestones may already be too damaged because of age or neglect, so cleaning them would require a specialist.

In some cases, the gravestone may need to be completely replaced. Sometimes memorial companies can incorporate a piece of the old gravestone into a new design, which is a nice touch for keeping the energy of the original memorial intact.

SAFETY AND SPIRITUAL PROTECTION

If you ask any person who does spirit work—whether that is in the form of an ancestor practice or paranormal investigation work—they will likely have their own views on cemeteries and the spirits who occupy them.

One of the main beliefs people have is that ghosts and spirits don't spend time in cemeteries because there isn't enough energy from the living for them to draw upon in order to manifest.

I humbly disagree with this idea.

Cemeteries are some of the most alive places there are; you just need to know where to look.

If you close your eyes and picture your favorite cemetery, what do you see? I see trees, grass, and blooming flowers. I see animals and birds, I see people jogging and people mourning. I see an abundance of life.

Even cemeteries and graveyards that are closed to new burials or ones that have been abandoned are overflowing with energy. Their wildness contributes to their power.

Another popular belief is that cemeteries attract "evil" spirits looking to harm people, and that any magical workings should be avoided there.

There are a few problems with this idea.

The first is that it perpetuates the notion that this type of work is inherently evil or harmful.

This belief often also stems from problematic depictions in popular culture about African diasporic religions, as well as Indigenous American spirituality.

If there were as many negative hauntings and demonic possessions out there as the satanic panic would have us believe, we would be in serious trouble.

Of course, there is a risk of encountering something that is uncomfortable. There is even a chance that you will encounter something harmful. Not only is that true of any spiritual practice, but it's true of the living world as well.

But by not visiting the cemetery, or by bringing these types of fears into the environment, you're missing out on valuable lessons and the opportunity to grow your ancestor practice.

However, when going into any realm of the dead, you still want to be prepared both physically and spiritually. Working with the dead should be approached with a certain amount of seriousness and respect.

Physical safety

The most obvious danger lurking in the cemetery is the threat of physical harm... from falling headstones.

The weight of a headstone or monument can be deadly. Never attempt to move or reset a stone yourself. If you believe a monument is at risk of toppling over, be sure to let the cemetery staff know.

Before any cemetery excursion, you must research the location.

Is the cemetery currently maintained or has it been abandoned? An abandoned graveyard can contain more risks, such as tripping hazards, poisonous plants, and venomous animals.

Always follow the rules posted by the cemetery. If they aren't available online, ask at the office, or call and ask. If the cemetery is abandoned, try checking with the city or town where it's located, as they may have ownership of the property.

If the cemetery is by appointment only, make an appointment. Do not trespass.

Follow safety signs and stay out of restricted areas.

If you are not actively looking at stones, be sure to stay on marked paths. The earth in cemeteries can be loose from digging, increased moisture, and uneven weight distribution from monuments.

Respect the guidelines for offerings and decorations.

If they say not to bring glass or burn candles, do not bring them. Find an alternative; LED candles can be bought almost anywhere these days at an affordable price.

If you would like to plant flowers or shrubs, be sure you follow the planting guidelines. These can usually be found online; if not, be sure to call and ask. Nothing feels worse than planting something only to come back to find it dug up.

Be respectful of mourners.

An active burial will always take precedence over your visit. If you will be a distraction to a funeral, come back another time.

Keep your voice low and don't stare.

Spiritual safety

The cemetery is like a city.

The different sections are essentially different neighborhoods or communities. The plots themselves are the houses and apartment buildings. There are rules and "laws" the spirits are expected to follow during interactions—not only with one another but with the living as well.

And while cities are generally safe, they aren't immune to violence or petty crime. When you have a large group of people together in one area, you're bound to have the occasional problem.

Use common sense.

Do your research. Seek out the stories, local lore, and history not only of the cemetery, but of the land it is located on as well.

If a cemetery or graveyard is well-known for having a lot of "negative" spiritual activity, you should be extra cautious in your work there.

That doesn't mean you can't engage with the cemetery and the spirits within, but you should keep to yourself and to your ancestors.

Don't make yourself a target.

Most issues that do arise in cemeteries and with spirit work are the result of a visitor taunting or bothering the spirits in some way.

You wouldn't go up to random people in the street and start getting in their business or behaving in an antagonistic way, so don't do it in a cemetery. It's rude and inappropriate.

As in a city, most people and spirits at the cemetery are doing their own thing and aren't concerned with you. You may occasionally come across a "nosy neighbor," but they are typically harmless. It's up to you to decide what you're comfortable with.

Be firm in your boundaries.

In chapter 3 we went over spiritual boundaries; bring these to the cemetery with you.

Enter the cemetery with confidence, but always be respectful. Remember that you are a guest in this space and that trying to change the way things work won't be appreciated.

Ask the cemetery guardian for protection.

If you've been building a relationship with this spirit (chapter 3), ask them to watch over you.

Pay your cemetery fee or perform an act of service (pages 6–7).

Ask your ancestor for protection.

This is one of the best things you can do to feel safe and secure. It is in your ancestor's best interests that you remain both happy and healthy.

Wear or carry a protective amulet.

As discussed in chapter 3, having an external form of protection can help provide you with security.

CEMETERY SPIRITS

An array of spirits call the cemetery home, and each place will be different. No matter where you visit, understand that it takes time to build a relationship with both the grounds and the spirits who live there. You may have a connection due to having family buried there, but you still must do the work.

Human spirits of the cemetery

The first and most important occupants of a cemetery are the spirits who are buried there. As I mentioned earlier, you will want to think of the cemetery as a city, with the different sections acting as the neighborhoods. Some families have all their graves in one neighborhood, while others can be spread out across many neighborhoods. When we—the living—are in the cemetery, we are taking on the role of tourists. It is important that we remain respectful and nondisruptive to the places we visit.

As in living cities, the spirits in a large cemetery may be more receptive to visitors, whereas a small single-family graveyard may not be as welcoming. A stranger walking into a family graveyard would be like a stranger walking into your front yard or apartment building. There are times when this is acceptable, such as mail delivery, and there are times when it is disruptive, such as door-to-door recruitment. Don't be the door-to-door salesman of the cemetery.

Many people in the paranormal community believe that the cemetery does not contain spirits of the dead who are buried there. They argue that they would rather be at their childhood home or another important location...but why is the resting place of their body (or cremains) and a monument in their name *not* considered an important location?

I covered spirit anchors in the ancestor altar chapter (chapter 4), but I believe the spirits of the dead can move in ways that we cannot. Their energy can be in multiple places at once. I believe spirits do spend a lot of time in the cemetery (or places where their cremains are spread).

As you spend more time in the cemetery, you will notice that there are certain areas or even certain gravestones that you feel drawn to. Performing acts of service or providing offerings to the spirits in these neighborhoods can help you build a stronger relationship with the entire cemetery community.

One important thing to remember is that in any cemetery, there may be human spirits who have been there since long before it was built. The cemetery could be located on land that they owned or tended, or perhaps they traveled through it on a regular basis.

In Ireland and the UK, many of the early Christian monasteries and church graveyards were built on or near existing Celtic sites so that the clergy could convert people more easily.

Researching both the cemetery and the land it occupies will provide you with a better understanding of the spirits you may encounter.

The cemetery guardian

One figure in the cemetery that I urge you to become acquainted with is the cemetery guardian.

Though most often the guardian is a human spirit, they may be a nonhuman entity as well.

All cemeteries and graveyards have a guardian spirit. Their role is to protect the cemetery grounds and the other spirits who reside there.

On a spiritual level, they keep things running smoothly. Think of them as the overseer of operations.

In English folklore, they are known as the church grim or kirk grim. This belief was likely brought to the British Isles from Scandinavia, where they are known as the kyrkogrim (Swedish) and kirkegrim (Danish).

In some stories, the cemetery guardian is described as fierce and dangerous, while in others they appear as stern but welcoming. Each cemetery guardian is unique, and how you approach and interact with each one will be different every time.

Who is the cemetery guardian and how are they chosen?

In most cases, the cemetery guardian is the spirit of a once-living person. Older folklore states that the first person interred in the cemetery becomes the guardian, and this is left entirely to chance.

In order to circumvent this, many communities would bury a dog or other animal on the grounds in the hopes that it would then become the guardian. Some historians believe that it is also possible that a person could be chosen for the role and buried alive.

In some areas of Scotland, it was thought that the role of guardian moved from person to person. With each new burial the torch would be passed. This belief raises an interesting question: if a cemetery falls out of use, does the last person buried remain the guardian forever?

The most obvious candidate for the cemetery guardian is the sexton or other staff. Who better to take on the guardian role in the spirit world than the people who performed it in life?

There is a type of intimacy between the people who work at the cemetery and those who are buried there. These staff members are the ones who ensure that people are interred correctly, and that their families are treated compassionately. They watch over the landscape and animals and make sure that everyone stays safe.

The first thing you should do when trying to build a relationship with the guardian is research. There is no room for skipping steps in a spirit practice, and acclimating to the cemetery is no exception.

The following prompts can help you get started:

- What year was the cemetery created?
- What date did it open for burials?
- Who was the first burial? If the cemetery was opened for burials in May 1900, but the earliest death comes up as March 1900, it is possible that that person was moved from their original location.
- Who were the original caretakers?
- Who was the architect?
- What folklore or stories surround the cemetery?
- What was the land used for before it was a cemetery?

Greyfriars Bobby—the guardian of Greyfriars Kirkyard

On the corner of Candlemakers Row in Edinburgh, Scotland, overlooking the famous Greyfriars Kirkyard, stands the most photographed statue in the entire city.

This bronze figure and water fountain memorializes a little Skye Terrier named Greyfriars Bobby, who is considered by most to be the guardian of the graveyard.

How did this little dog find himself with this sacred duty? Well, that story begins with his owner.

In 1850 a landscaper named John Gray moved his family to Edinburgh for new financial opportunities. Unfortunately, John struggled to obtain work as a gardener, as he had hoped.

In a last-ditch effort to avoid the workhouses—sweatshops rife with abuse and disease—Gray became a police constable. Policing the city during the night shift was a difficult and an undesirable job, but Gray saw it as the lesser of two evils.

Though he had avoided the workhouse, the long, cold nights and unhealthy conditions of Edinburgh took their toll, and not long after starting his job, Gray was diagnosed with tuberculosis. Over the next few months his condition deteriorated, and he died.

From the moment he was interred in Greyfriars Kirkyard, his dog, Bobby, was there to watch over him.

Rain or shine, Bobby lay on top of Gray's grave, much to the dismay of the sexton, James Brown. But as the months and years passed, Brown warmed to the little dog and built him a small shelter near the grave to live in.

On occasion, Bobby would follow another man, John Traill, to the coffee-house he owned for a midday meal. But even though the little dog trusted Traill, he would never leave the graveyard for long.

He belonged to it as much as it belonged to him.

As time moved on, Bobby became a bit of a local celebrity. The residents of Edinburgh were very protective of him, so when a local bylaw threatened his life, people were understandably distraught.

You see, all dogs in Edinburgh were required to be licensed, and with his owner deceased, Bobby had nobody to cover his fee.

Thankfully, the Lord Provost, Sir William Chambers, heard his tale, and it touched his heart. He paid the licensing fee for Bobby and even bought him a collar engraved with his information.

It is currently on display at the Museum of Edinburgh.

GREYFRIARS BOBBY FROM THE LORD PROVOST—1867—LICENSED.

For fourteen years, Bobby faithfully watched over John Gray's grave, until Wednesday, January 17, 1872, when an article appeared in *The Scotsman* announcing the dog's death.

Many will be sorry to hear that the poor but interesting dog 'Greyfriars Bobby' died on Sunday evening. Every kind attention was paid to him in his last days by his guardian Mr. Traill who has had him buried in a flower pot near Greyfriars Church. His collar, a gift from the Lord Provost Chambers, has been deposited in the office at the church gate. Mr. Brodie has successfully modelled the figure of Greyfriars Bobby which is to be erected by the munificence of the Baroness Burdett Coutts.

It is that very statue commissioned by the baroness that rests on the corner, visited day after day by locals and tourists alike.

But that isn't the only monument erected in Bobby's honor.

In Greyfriars Kirkyard itself, a gravestone greets you as you enter.

Greyfriars Bobby
Died 14th January 1872
Aged 16 Years
Let his loyalty and devotion
Be a lesson to us all

Every few years, an article surfaces questioning the validity of Bobby's story, but that hasn't stopped his legend from growing.

Death hasn't seemed to put an end to Bobby's activities, either. Many people have claimed to catch a glimpse of the ghostly terrier making the after-lunch run back to Greyfriars, where offerings of sticks lie loyally at his grave.

GRAVE OFFERINGS

For as long as humans have been burying the dead, we have been providing them with the tools they need to live well on the other side. One of the ways we do that is in the form of **grave goods**—ritual and practical items that are buried in, or laid in the vicinity of, the grave.

And just as we have given the dead practical items, we have also given them mementos and gifts in the form of **grave offerings** to pay tribute to and honor them.

Grave offerings are a wonderful way to bond with your ancestors. Taking the time to visit and bond with departing family at their resting place is an act of love.

While you don't need a specific occasion to leave an offering, it can be helpful to incorporate visits into holidays for extra spiritual energy.

Flower offerings

Here do ye find us steady in our trust,
As sentinels who stand to guard the dead.
Each has her charge to watch the sacred dust,
Of someone sleeping in the dreamless bed.

Flowers are some of the most common grave offerings you will find in a cemetery. This excerpt from the poem "The Flowers in the Cemetery" by Hannah Flagg Gould highlights their sacred duty to protect and comfort the dead.

The ancient Egyptians loved to arrange all sorts of flower bouquets for a wide variety of occasions. One common use was for funerals, and after the person was interred, the flowers would be left at the site as a tribute.

The ancient Greeks and Romans also used flowers to honor people. Flowers would be left atop the graves of warriors, and it was thought that if the flowers took root in the soil, the person's soul had found peace on the other side.

And of course, during the Victorian era, flowers had a massive rise in popularity. An entire symbolic language was created about them, which is still often referenced today. With the rise of the garden cemetery, flowers and graves became even more intertwined.

Most cultures have flowers that are associated with spirits and the dead, so for your practice, it's best to begin by exploring your own heritage. If you still aren't sure which flowers to start with, you really can't go wrong with the classics: lilies, roses, chrysanthemums, carnations, gladiolas, daffodils, marigolds, and hydrangeas are all beautiful and can be procured easily.

Tip: It is not part of Jewish tradition to leave flowers on graves, but the custom is growing in popularity. You may wish to check with the local synagogue about what is appropriate. When in doubt, don't offer flowers.

There are many different ways you can offer flowers at a grave, and ways to incorporate them afterward into your practice. I will be covering two rituals that I created specifically for this book.

You may wish to perform your own ritual instead as you see fit.

Flower Sentinel Spell

The first of the two options is to perform the Flower Sentinel Spell.

This is a good choice for those who may not be able to visit the cemetery as often as they'd like.

What you need

- Cemetery planting guidelines
- Permission to plant (from the cemetery and the plot owner)
- Perennial flowers
- A spade
- Your intention
- A waxing moon in spring

Don't forget to record everything in your BOA!

Steps

The first step of this spell is to obtain permission to plant from both the cemetery office and the plot owner, and then to acquire a copy of the planting guidelines.

Next, look into which perennial you'd like to plant. Your research should include practical information like the planting zone, weather, and sun exposure requirements.

It should also include spiritual elements such as color association, metaphysical meaning, and personal taste (both yours and the deceased's).

I would also urge you to focus on planting native flower species whenever possible.

After you have picked out your flower and obtained permission, you will want to find a day in the spring during the waxing moon period to plant.

If you live somewhere cold, this should be after the frost warning has been lifted for the year.

When you arrive at the cemetery, inform the guardian of your plan and make your way to your ancestor's location.

As you begin arranging and planning where each flower sentinel will go, talk to your ancestor.

Explain to them why you chose these specific flowers, and how you hope they offer protection and comfort.

The next step is to begin digging. As you do, take notice of your feelings.

Digging in a cemetery can be an intense experience because of its liminal nature.

Allow whatever feelings come up to be there with you. Don't try to stifle your emotions.

When you're ready, start placing the flowers in their new home.

As you do, tell them out loud the purpose for which they are being planted there.

You may even opt to read the entire "Flowers in the Cemetery" poem out loud as you plant. It is freely available online.

Writing this intention down and placing it in the earth under the flowers can add a little extra power to the spell. Use a biodegradable, unbleached paper.

When you have finished the spell, take some time to reflect and admire your work.

Now would be a great time to take some photographs for your BOA or try some divination.

ADAMS

Adams Ellen S
12 | 1075

1489

Single G 1641

WHERE INTER

SEC. L

8   55
Childs Single 179 dees
"   "   178 Case

10   250
Childs Pon Inter 56
12   403 N½ Con 24
8   354
11   168 S½
10   54
12   53 & Equor
12   1075
10   277
12   71 & outoff
10   443 malt
Childs Pon Inter 56
12   1025 N½
8   356
10   370
Childs Pon Inter 56
"   "   " 56
Adult Single Grave 11
10   490
Childs Pon Inter 56
"   "   " 56
12   1065 N½
10   300
10   188

Pressed grave flower wards

This next ritual is a way to offer flowers to your ancestor, create a protection spell for your home, and craft a lovely keepsake for your descendants.

> **Don't forget to record everything in your BOA!**

What you need

- Flowers
- Sheets of watercolor paper
- Heavy books
- A double glass frame
- A hot-glue gun

First-half steps

This first half of the ritual is all about the physical act of offering flowers to your ancestor at the cemetery or other resting place.

First things first: you need to choose an ancestor to honor with a flower offering.

If you have many ancestors in the same cemetery, you may wish to leave a single flower at each grave.

Next you will choose the flower type you'd like to use.

The "Flora: plants of the dead" section later in this chapter can be used to help you pick; if you know the favorite flower of the deceased, you can use that.

And finally, choose an appropriate date for the offering.

Birthdays, death days, and other anniversaries are great options because they are personal, but if you follow the Wheel of the Year, you may wish to make the offering during a Sabbat. You can learn more about Sabbats on pages 273–75.

When you arrive at the cemetery, greet the guardian before making your way to your ancestor's grave.

Now it is time to make your offering.

This step is very personal, and you should do what feels right for you. I like to explain to my ancestor why I chose a particular flower for them.

Keep one flower for yourself.

Because some gravestones can be susceptible to damage—especially limestone—I like to place the flower at the base of the stone.

Be sure to remove any litter or plastic material and make a plan to return and tidy up in a few weeks. Cemetery staff will usually clean the cemetery at least twice a season, but it isn't always guaranteed.

Back at your home, place the flower you kept on your ancestor altar in a vase of water for a few days.

Second-half steps

The second half of the ritual is when we craft the protection ward and keepsake. The flowers you leave as offerings can be used for powerful protection in your home. Not only do they contain the cemetery energy, your ancestor's energy, and your altar's energy, but the flowers themselves also have their own energy.

Building this project takes time because you are using a flower from each visit. You need to build up a stash of them.

Before the flower you kept from your visit begins to wilt, remove it from the vase and pat it dry with a tissue.

Next, layer two sheets of watercolor paper on a flat surface. Watercolor paper is ideal because it is highly absorbent.

Place your flower on the paper and cover it with another two sheets of paper.

Carefully stack a couple of heavy books on top of the paper. Do not touch it for one week.

After one week, carefully remove the books and check on the flower to evaluate how dry it is. It will likely need another two or three weeks until it's completely dry.

Move the flower—gently—to a new piece of paper and repeat the process.

Once you have a nice collection of dried grave flowers, it's time to start putting them together in the frame.

Begin arranging the flowers on the glass of the frame in a way that looks aesthetically pleasing to you.

You may need a small dot of hot glue to secure the flowers in place.

One you have a design you like, place the other piece of glass on top and secure it.

Hang your new protection ward near your ancestor altar or by your front door.

Additional ideas

You may wish to make a frame for each ancestor.

You could also include a photo of your ancestor or the gravestone in the frame.

Don't forget to document the process in your BOA and write whom you would like to inherit this keepsake.

> TIP: If you do not have access to the cemetery where your ancestors are buried, you can leave virtual flowers with a message on findagrave.com.

Money offerings

Money is an important offering in the cemetery. It is the literal embodiment of "paying your respects."

Money is both practical and highly symbolic. We use it every day to buy the things we need.

We put a lot of energy into earning money, so when you give the gift of money to both the cemetery guardian and your ancestors, you are showing that you value them.

I recommend leaving a coin at the entrance of the cemetery gate for the guardian at each visit, especially if you're just getting to know each other.

Donating to a cemetery protection and conservation fund is a great way to show you are serious about putting in the necessary effort to build a relationship with the cemetery spirits. Some graveyards will have their own donation system in place, but if not, check with your local historical or genealogical societies.

There is a long tradition in both the USA and parts of Canada of leaving coins on the gravestones of servicepeople. If you have an ancestor who was in the military, they may appreciate an offering of coins.

In some cases, different denominations can mean different things.

Penny: means you visited the gravestone and want to show your respect
Nickel: means you attended boot camp together
Dime: means you served together
Quarter: means you were present when they died

Canada has actually abolished the use of pennies, so it will be interesting to see how this tradition evolves.

In most cases, you can't go wrong leaving coins on the gravestones of your ancestors; however, be aware that coins can rust and permanently mark the stone.

Rock and gemstone offerings

The act of leaving rocks and pebbles on headstones is a Jewish custom. Traditionally, at the end of each visit to the grave, a pebble is selected and placed on top of the headstone.

The exact origin of the practice is unknown, but there are some popular theories as to how it originated. One is that it began as a way of tethering the recently departed soul to earth as they adjust to their new reality. Another is that it prevents any golem—a creature from Jewish folklore that is formed out of clay—from getting into the grave.

These days, however, placing a pebble on the top of a Jewish gravestone is a sign of respect and a welcome gesture.

Modern witches have also adopted the practice of leaving rocks and gemstones on gravestones as offerings.

Different gemstones carry different meanings:

Rose quartz: love, beauty, and comfort
Clear quartz: manifesting, divination, and cleansing

Black tourmaline: grounding, protection, and banishing
Amethyst: clairvoyance, psychic ability, and mental clarity
Citrine: money, abundance, and creativity
Aventurine: confidence, luck, and abundance
Cyanite: removing negativity, connection, and dreams
Pyrite: money, inspiration, and protection
Bloodstone: building connections, balance, and improving memory
Obsidian: protection, spiritual growth, and absorbing negativity

> Caution: It is important to do your research when sourcing your gemstones. Mining is a highly exploitative industry when it comes to human rights and environmental impact. Make sure you source your gemstones responsibly.

Shell offerings

Though today shells on graves are a common sight in coastal cities and towns, in the USA their origin lies in the Black cemeteries of the South.

Enslaved people from the Bakongo region would leave conch shells on graves in the belief that the shell would protect the soul as it traveled across the river to the other side, where eternal life awaited.

And, as we learned earlier, these shells were not just offerings in some cases— they were the grave markers themselves.

Written accounts from the 1800s state that the shells would be cleaned and bleached white either by the sun or by household cleaners available at the time.

Conch shells can be purchased easily today, but you may feel it's more significant to collect and clean your own.

How to clean shells:

Fill a bucket or basin with warm water and a drop of dish soap.

Immerse your shells in the sudsy mixture and let them soak for ten minutes.

Next, take a soft toothbrush and gently scrub off any tough debris.

When the shells look sufficiently clean, rinse them well with fresh water.

If you'd like to brighten up the shells a little, you can try bleaching them.

Mix one part water and one part bleach and let the shells soak for about thirty minutes.

Use rubber gloves when removing the shells from the water. Rinse thoroughly and allow to dry.

Personalized offerings

With any type of ancestor practice and grave offering, you can never go wrong with something personal. Your ancestors had pastimes just as you do, and it will mean a lot to them to receive a little token relating to their interests.

As long as the items are not against the cemetery rules or harmful to the wildlife, you can be creative with this.

Time offerings

An offering that is usually overlooked by new practitioners is simply spending time with your ancestors in the cemetery.

Even though it can't really be measured monetarily, time is still precious. What you do while at the cemetery doesn't always need to be an involved ritual. Simply sitting and talking to your ancestors or reading them books can mean more than all the flowers in the world.

CEMETERY KIT

For genealogists and tombstone tourists, the key to any successful graveyard or cemetery adventure is making sure you are well prepared for your visit.

Here are the essentials I keep in my cemetery kit. Feel free to modify this list to suit your personal needs.

Backpack: The first item to go into your cemetery kit is its container—a backpack. If you plan on doing many excursions, you will want to buy yourself a lightweight one with good shoulder support and lots of storage room.

Water and snacks: If you're anything like me, your graveyard excursions will often last a lot longer than intended, so you will want to have water and snacks on hand.

Proper footwear and long pants: While in the cemetery, the last thing you want is to break a toe on a loose headstone or to have poison ivy brush up against your bare legs. Long pants and sturdy shoes are a must.

Gloves: If you come across a headstone that needs to be cleared of debris, or you're collecting litter for your act of service (pages 225–27), a pair of gardening gloves can really come in handy.

Sunscreen and bug spray: It should go without saying, but your skin should be thoroughly protected from the sun's harmful rays. Bug spray or tick repellent is also good to have if the graveyard is overgrown.

Plastic bag: You should always leave a cemetery cleaner than you found it. If there are no garbage bins on-site, carrying a receptacle for litter is a good idea.

Soft bristle brush: A soft brush can help you clear away dirt from a head-stone. Be sure to remove only topical debris like loose leaves and sticks. Removing roots or lichen can compromise the integrity of the stone. A brush with hard bristles can damage or scratch older headstones.

Small spade: If you are planting flowers (or collecting graveyard dirt), a mini-spade is your best friend.

Please do not dig in a graveyard or cemetery without permission. Many cemeteries have flower planting guidelines on their websites or posted in the office.

Resealable poly bags: If you are collecting graveyard dirt, use small plastic bags with the name of the grave occupant and their location recorded on them.

Offerings: Always, always, always bring an appropriate offering for both the people you are visiting and the cemetery guardian (pages 208–10).

Map and rules: Almost all cemeteries and graveyards these days have a website where you can find a PDF map and a list of rules. If you are visiting an older graveyard that is no longer in use, you can probably find a map or land survey in the local archives.

Notebook and pen: I like to keep a small notebook with me for headstone descriptions, interesting epitaphs, and results of any divination I do, and to make notes about flora and fauna I find. All of these notes get transferred later to my BOA.

Mirror and flashlight: Headstones can be hard to read. Having a midsize hand mirror can help you reflect light into the shadows and make lettering more legible.

Divinatory tools: I love to do cemetery divination. Having a range of tools with me is imperative. Using more than one divinatory tool in a session, such as tarot cards and divining rods, allows me to play around or confirm hazy messages.

Spiritual protection: Cemeteries and graveyards are generally safe places, but it is always a good idea to wear or carry a talisman (pages 159–63).

EVP recorder: This tape recorder is the one piece of ghost-hunting equipment I carry everywhere. EVP stands for electronic voice phenomenon, which essentially means capturing a spirit voice on tape. You never know when the opportunity for a Scientific Séance will arise. (This is a type of séance you can learn more about in *The Book of Séances*.)

ACTS OF SERVICE

Seasonal cleanup

While many of the larger cemeteries and graveyards have caretakers who keep the grounds tidy and free from debris, many of the smaller ones—or those that are no longer in use—don't have that luxury.

At the start of each season, head to a cemetery in your area and help clean it up.

However, don't be overzealous—you might accidentally throw away another person's offerings or dedications to their loved ones!

If you come across mementos that have become separated from their gravestone, bring them to the cemetery office for safekeeping. If there is no office or designated area to put them in, leave them where they are. Chances are the person who left these items will be back to look for them.

Get involved in conservation

One of the best ways to give back to your community is to get involved with cemetery conservation. There are many different organizations working to ensure these places are protected, and they can always use your help.

The easiest way to pitch in is to make a donation to your local historical or genealogical society. Most have a dedicated cemetery fund that is spent on a specific restoration project each year. You might also consider becoming a member so that you have a say in how that money is spent.

In the USA and Canada, Black cemeteries face many threats, such as vandalism and neglect, and are at an increased risk of being destroyed to make way for new housing and commercial developments.

The Black Cemetery Network was created to protect and restore these cemeteries, and the network's website shares much information about how people can help either by donating, educating themselves, or volunteering their time.

Indigenous burial grounds also face desecration and are at increased risk of being destroyed due to developments, pipelines, and deforestation. Indigenous land defenders are often arrested for protecting these sacred places.

The National Centre for Truth and Reconciliation in Canada and the Association on American Indian Affairs in the USA offer a wealth of information on how people can help either by donating, educating themselves, or volunteering their time.

Volunteer for Find a Grave or BillionGraves

Getting involved with one of the cemetery documentation websites is a great way to earn favor with the cemetery spirits.

Each time you're at the cemetery, take a minute to search the graves in your vicinity. They may already have photos posted, but if they are older or not of great quality you should update them.

> TIP: Ask permission or inform the spirit of your plan before you photograph their gravestone.

HEADSTONE SYMBOLS DICTIONARY

When you first begin to explore the cemetery, you'll be greeted by a host of imagery and iconography woven among the graves. There is a story to be found here, and learning the language carved in the stones is important for both your genealogy journey and your ancestor magic practice.

Understanding the symbols you discover will allow you to interpret the messages left for you by your ancestors. These inscriptions can give insight into how religious a person was, whether they were optimistic or fearful about what was waiting for them on the other side, whether they believed in reincarnation, and even what their occupation was in life.

The following dictionary contains some of the most popular symbols found in the cemetery. I have divided them into the categories of flora, fauna, objects, and human as a jumping-off point for your studies.

Flora: plants of the dead

All living things have a spirit, and this includes the plants and trees you encounter in the cemetery. Plants play an integral role in magic and ancestor work, as their spirits belong to both the living and the dead.

Even the most manicured of burial grounds will have an abundance of different species you must get to know.

Keep a record of the tree and plant species in close proximity to your ancestors' gravestones, as well as those engraved on their headstones.

These plants can be incorporated into your spells and rituals to help boost connection.

Acanthus leaves: Often used in cemetery architecture, these leaves represent the "prickly" or difficult parts of life. However, they do offer hope about what is waiting for a person on the other side because of their strong associations with immortality in ancient Greek culture.

Acorn or oak leaves: A symbol of spirituality. Someone who lived a humble life or showed strength and determination.

Anemone: According to Greek mythology, anemone flowers grew from the tears Aphrodite cried upon the grave of Adonis. These blooms represent sincerity, beauty, and everlasting love.

Bellflower: There is a wide range of bellflower species, but on a headstone, most of them represent sorrow and mourning. Their shape is indicative of the "dead bell" that was rung at the head of a funeral procession.

Buttercup: These delicate yellow flowers represent the sweetness and innocence of youth. They often indicate that the grave belongs to a child or someone who died well before their time.

Calla lily: This elegant flower not only represents marriage and passion but also can symbolize resurrection and the purity of soul.

Chrysanthemum: Chrysanthemums are indicative of hardiness and longevity, as they can survive in colder temperatures. In Japan, the chrysanthemum represents the sun, mortality, and happiness.

Clover: When in the three-leaved formation known as the shamrock, the clover represents the Holy Trinity, as well as Irish identity. A four-leaf clover symbolizes someone who was lucky or blessed in life.

Cyprus tree: Cypress trees are associated with death in many European and Muslim countries. The tree's cone shape is believed to point toward the heavens. The Greeks and Romans believed that a cypress was the first thing a person would see upon entering the Underworld. These trees are also thought to be immortal, as they can withstand a lot of damage.

Daffodil: Also known as narcissus, the daffodil has a wide range of associations: love, devotion, vanity, youth, innocence, triumph, and sacrifices.

Daisy: In medieval and early modern Britain, a daisy-like symbol known as a hexafoil would be carved into the walls and beams of a house or a church for protection. The daisy is also used as a divinatory tool around the world: questioners pick petals off the flower as a means of predicting love or how many children they may have. And of course, daisies are a symbol of death. When someone dies, it is said they are "pushing up daisies." On a headstone, a daisy can represent the death of a child, innocence, simplicity, protection, and sweetness.

Elm tree: In Greek mythology, the first elm trees were grown after the legendary musician Orpheus rescued his wife, Eurydice, from the Underworld. The infamous Tyburn gallows in England were nicknamed the elms or the triple tree, as elm trees in the area were used for hangings before the gallows' construction. The saying "sent to the elms" meant you were being sent to your death.

Evening primrose: This wildflower commonly grows in rural North American graveyards, so it has naturally become associated with death. On a headstone it represents eternal love, remembrance, and hope.

> TIP: An evening primrose picked from a cemetery can aid in divination and spirit communication.

Evergreens: Evergreens of all varieties represent immortality and the traveling of souls. A graveyard favorite, evergreen trees are not only found on headstones, but are often planted in the cemetery to act as spiritual guardians.

Ferns: When seen on headstones, ferns are references to sincerity and having a humble nature, but ferns have a rich symbolic history around the world. For the Maori they represent new life and fresh beginnings. In Japan they can symbolize hope and optimism.

Grapes: Grapes and grapevines symbolize fertility, prosperity, and abundance. They are also associated with the blood of Christ and souls being absolved of their sins in the afterlife.

Hawthorn: Hawthorn trees have long been associated with love and marriage in the Celtic world. In the British Isles, they bloom in May and are associated with the Gaelic festival of Beltane. On a headstone they represent love and union in marriage.

Holly: The Druids associated holly with divinity and eternal life. One American folk belief says that holly on a headstone will protect it from lightning.

Ivy: Ivy is a fitting symbol for a headstone, since it represents rebirth and regeneration. Ivy can often be found growing on headstones, slowly reclaiming them into the land.

Laurel: For the Romans, laurel was indicative of glory and mastery. To be given a laurel wreath was a high honor. In headstone symbolism, laurel speaks of eternity, prestige, and a blessed soul.

Lichen: Because lichen makes its home on headstones, it is naturally one of the most abundant grave symbols there is. While lichen does cause damage, on occasion it can protect the surface of a gravestone. If lichen is growing on a porous material such as limestone, it may actually shield the stone from water and erosion.

Lily of the valley: Like the calla lily and the Madonna lily, the lily of the valley is a favorite in funerary art and motif. On a headstone, these lilies represent renewal, rebirth, and purity. They also symbolize a soul at peace.

Madonna lily: Also known as an Easter lily, this flower evokes an array of feelings. It is thought that these blooms were first used in funerals because their strong fragrance was capable of masking the odor of death. The Madonna lily on a headstone symbolizes purity and eternity.

Marigold: In Victorian headstone motif, this flower represents grief and sorrow. In Mexican culture, marigolds are associated with Día de los Muertos—the Day of the Dead. During this time, bright-orange marigolds adorn graves and ancestral altars. Their scent is believed to guide the spirits back home.

Poppy: The poppy is most often associated with the grave of a soldier. During November in Canada, the Royal Canadian Legion sells poppy pins that are worn on coats and tops until the eleventh (Remembrance Day). It is traditional to visit a cemetery that day and place a poppy on the grave of a World War I veteran as an offering.

Rose: No flower has captivated our hearts and minds more than the rose. The juxtaposition of the rose's beauty and its thorns appears in countless literary works. On a headstone, a rose can be used to mark the grave of a woman. A rosebud or rose with a broken stem signals the resting place of an infant or someone who died too young. Other meanings are beauty, eternity, love, and mortality.

Thistle: Thistles are the national flower of Scotland, so engraved on a headstone they can indicate Scottish heritage, but because of religious associations they can also represent sorrow and crucifixion.

Wheat: A sheaf of wheat, or wheat with a hand sickle, can represent living a long life. Wheat stalks are also symbolic of someone of Ukrainian heritage.

Willow: The weeping willow was a favorite of the Victorians and can be found on countless headstones as well as in cemetery gardens. Willows represent the Underworld, and their cascading branches symbolize our heads bowed in grief and silence.

Yew tree: Yew trees are heavily associated with death and the afterlife, particularly in the UK. It was once believed that a yew planted on a plague victim's grave would help purify the deceased. Areas already containing a yew tree were likely chosen to be burial lands because of their spiritual associations with the ancient pagan groups of Europe.

Fauna

Another form of spirit you are certain to encounter in the cemetery is the animal and insect variety.

As cities and towns have grown, many animals have taken refuge inside cemeteries. In Toronto, our garden cemeteries are home to deer, foxes, coyotes, squirrels, rabbits, raccoons, and countless bird and insect species.

Always be respectful of animals' space and take special care not to bring offerings that may hurt or poison our animal friends.

Bee: Bees are symbols of craftsmanship and community. A headstone with a bee or hive symbolizes a person who contributed greatly to their community. Bees can also be used to represent Christianity and the Virgin Mary.

Bird: Long believed to have the ability to move between worlds, birds on headstones represent the human spirit and its journey to heaven. The type of bird can offer additional meanings.

Butterfly: The butterfly is the ultimate symbol of resurrection and transformation. It symbolizes the soul of a person moving from one state of being to another. In recent years, butterflies have become a popular choice for the graves of children, as they represent peace and beauty.

Cat: A cat on a headstone is typically used to mark the grave of a beloved pet in an animal cemetery. If seen in a human cemetery, it generally means the person really liked cats. In most cultures cats are viewed negatively and therefore are uncommon symbols for a headstone.

Dog: Like the cat, a dog on a headstone is often reserved for someone cherishing a pet or displaying their love for the animal, but it can also symbolize loyalty, devotion, and a friendly personality.

Dove: Doves on headstones have multiple meanings, the most important being peace and tranquility. A dove depicted flying downward represents the Holy Spirit, but a dove flying upward signifies that the grave occupant's soul has ascended to heaven.

Lamb: When it comes to headstones, lambs generally mark the grave of a child. They symbolize innocence, purity, and youth.

Lion: Lions are indicative of courage, pride, and family legacy. They are often found on mausoleums and tombs acting as a protective figure—much like a gargoyle on a castle.

Pelican: One popular myth people once believed was that when food was scarce, pelicans would sometimes pierce their own chests and feed their blood to their young in order to ensure their survival. Naturally this motif on a headstone represents sacrifice and undying love.

Pegasus or winged horse: As a mythological creature, the winged horse or Pegasus is an interesting choice for a headstone decoration. It depicts resurrection and rebirth of the soul. The grave occupant may also have been whimsical and fond of literature.

Phoenix: Legends surrounding the phoenix can be found around the world. On Christian graves the phoenix symbolizes death and the subsequent resurrection, which leads to rebirth. In China, the phoenix is sometimes used to symbolize a happy marriage and longevity, as well as luck and harmony.

Snake: Prior to the 1900s, snakes were a prominent headstone symbol. They represent mortality and sin, as well as rebirth and regeneration. The image of a snake consuming its own tail—known as an ouroboros—dates all the way back to ancient Egypt and ancient Rome. The ouroboros symbolizes the cycle of life. In contrast, two snakes wrapped around a rod with wings is known as a caduceus, a symbol that dates back to the ancient Greeks. In North America this symbol represents medicine and therefore is placed on the graves of doctors and surgeons.

Objects

Anchor: Commonly found in seaside towns, an anchor on a headstone can signal the grave of a sailor. When the anchor appears upside down it can be a sign that the grave is empty because the person was lost at sea. In some regions, anchors also represent the Christian faith.

Arrow: The arrow is a symbol of the Death archetype. While most of us picture the Grim Reaper with a scythe, he also sometimes pierces people with the arrow of death.

Bell: The dead bell (also known as the mort, deid, or lych bell) represents the bell rung to announce a death or funeral procession, so naturally a bell represents grief and sorrow. Bells also show faith in God and being in his protection.

Boat: A boat typically represents a journey. The occupant has finished their voyage on earth and is ready for their next voyage, into the afterlife. A boat can also represent the grave of a sailor or someone who loved sailing.

Book: On a headstone, a book can have a variety of meanings, depending on how it is displayed. A closed book often indicates that the person lived a long, full life. They made it to the "last page," so to speak. An open book symbolizes a life cut short or death in middle age. Books in general represent the Bible or word of God, especially when they are paired with a crown.

Broken pillar: A broken pillar represents an abrupt end. When you see this type of headstone marker or engraving, you can assume the deceased died young.

Candle: One of the most enduring symbols of the human spirit, the candle speaks of hope and optimism. The number of candles depicted can offer additional clues. As do most groups of three objects, three candles represent the

Holy Trinity. Five candles can be a reference to the Crucifixion, and one candle can mean that the grave belongs to a Jewish woman. A solitary candle that is being snuffed out symbolizes life coming to an end.

Chair: An empty chair symbolizes the death of a young person, or a life that was cut down early or suddenly. It signifies that the person is "missing" from the world of the living.

Crook: The shepherd's crook means charity and community involvement. The crook can be found all over the ancient world and was common in Assyria, Babylonia, and Egypt—where it is a symbol of Osiris.

Cross: A symbol of Christianity. There are many different types of crosses around the world. Some are simple and in the classic T shape, while others, like the Celtic cross, incorporate a circle into the design.

Crown: A crown on a headstone means that the person in the grave has ascended to heaven. Crowns are also symbols of life and a person who lived well or had some sort of status in the community.

Cup: Cups and other vessels have long been associated with divinity and spiritual knowledge. Most cups symbolize Catholicism and the blood of Christ, but cups are not a uniquely Catholic image.

Curtain: The curtain or veil represents the spiritual boundary that divides the living and the dead. In death, the occupant has been granted the ability to travel between these realms. The curtain also represents the end of something—in this case, the end of a life.

> **TIP:** Pay special attention to a headstone that bears this symbol, as the boundary between the world of the living and world of the dead may be thinner here. It would make a good area to perform divination.

Gate: Like the veil and curtain, the gate is a symbol of moving from one realm to the next. It can also be a depiction of the gate to heaven.

Hammer: A hammer alone or with an anvil on a headstone typically means that the person worked as a blacksmith, a once-revered trade. If the person was not a blacksmith, they may have possessed a special skill or been a craftsman.

Harp: The harp is the national symbol of Ireland and therefore can represent the grave of a person from that country. The harp also can mean sweetness, grace, and finding the heavens.

Horseshoe: The horseshoe is a symbol of luck and prosperity. It can also symbolize a grave belonging to a professional jockey or horse lover. On older graves it can be another hint that the person was a blacksmith.

Hourglass: An hourglass represents the allotment of time each person is given on earth. Because an hourglass can be inverted, it also suggests that souls may reincarnate or be resurrected.

Key: Secrets, mysteries, and divine knowledge are represented by keys. The person in this grave is being given the key to the kingdom of heaven.

Ladder: Ladders on a headstone can symbolize many different things. They appear in Buddhist and Islamic cultures, as well as in Christianity. The Freemasons will sometimes use a three-rung ladder with the letters "CHF," which stand for charity, hope, and faith. If none of those situations applies to the person whom the grave belongs to, it could be just about their ascent to heaven or moving on to something better.

Menorah: A Jewish symbol that represents the presence of God. The menorah is often synonymous with feeling hopeful in a period of uncertainty.

Scale: Balance, fairness, and the law are symbolized by this image. A scale almost always adorns the resting place of a lawyer or judge.

Scythe: The scythe and the sickle are the most recognized tools of the Grim Reaper. Scythes are about "cutting down" or harvesting the souls of the living—a grim reminder that Death conquers all.

Sexton's tools: A sexton was a person who took care of the graveyard or cemetery. They were responsible for digging graves, general upkeep, and landscaping.

In larger cemeteries, the sexton took on a managerial role, whereas in smaller ones they typically performed the work themselves. If a headstone includes an image of a coffin surrounded by shovels, rakes, and other items of that nature, you are looking at the sexton's tools.

TIP: You may be standing before the cemetery guardian; be sure to leave an offering.

Star of David: The most recognizable symbol of Judaism found in a cemetery. It is protective in nature. It means the grave's occupant is protected from all six of the directions: north, south, east, west, up, and down.

Sun: The sun is the universal life-force. Without it, everything else ceases to exist. If depicted rising, the sun shows the beginning of a new state of being. If the sun is setting, it depicts an ending. The setting and rising sun look the same, so you'll need to use other symbols on the headstone to determine which it is.

Torch: An upside-down torch is found only in cemeteries and graveyards—you won't find it on buildings such as churches or museums. Like the candle, the flame of the torch represents life and the hope that life can somehow continue after death.

Urn: Urns represent the returning of the body to the earth. They became a popular decorative symbol in the nineteenth century, even though cremation was not very common at the time.

Human

Angel: Angels are usually, but not always, depicted with wings. These messengers of God can have a variety of meanings depending on how they are portrayed. A weeping angel represents sorrow and mourning. A praying angel symbolizes remaining steadfast in your faith in periods of turmoil or grief. If an angel is shown with a wreath, it signifies remembrance.

Death's-head: The death's-head is one of the most common symbols on European and American gravestones—especially in New England. The death's-head can

be depicted as a skull and crossbones, a skull with wings (usually angel or bird wings), a skull with sexton's tools, or even a child's or man's face with wings. The death's-head represents grief, despair, and mortality.

Father Time: Father Time is a figure from folklore who symbolizes the time each of us has on earth. Although he and the Grim Reaper are both associated with death, they are not the same.

Green man: The green man or "foliate head" is a figure found in many parts of Europe, but most often in Ireland and the UK. He is a pagan figure who symbolizes the new life that eventually comes from death. This figure can also act as a sort of protector or gargoyle archetype.

Grim Reaper: This well-known skeletal figure, who carries a scythe or an arrow, is a reminder that death comes for us all in the end.

Hands: Hands appear frequently in cemeteries and graveyards and can be deciphered based on what they are doing. A handshake between hands that look to be of different genders most often symbolizes a husband and wife. A handshake between two hands of the same gender represents brotherhood or friendship, but can also portray the deceased being welcomed to heaven. I like to believe that in some instances, handshakes between the same gender were hinting at an LGBTQ2S relationship. While we may never know for certain, this symbol paired with census information could possibly reveal whether the deceased likely cohabited with a same-sex partner. When a headstone shows a hand pointing up, it means the soul has ascended to heaven, while a hand pointing down surrounded by clouds is meant to show the hand of God. A hand pointing down sans clouds can mean an accidental death. Handshakes can also represent the living saying goodbye to the dead. Take a look at the fingers of each hand. If they look stiff and straight, then that is the hand of the deceased; if they are bent or in a clasping position, that is the hand of the living.

Hearts: The heart is a universal symbol of love, and it's no different when it appears on a headstone. A heart with ivy stands for enduring love and companionship. Two hearts stand for matrimony or an important relationship. Hearts on more modern graves often mark the resting place of a child.

Skulls, bones, and skeletons: In general, skeletons and bones serve as a reminder that we all eventually face the same fate: death.

Virtues: The seven virtues represent traits we find desirable in others and hope to embody ourselves. Most often the virtues are depicted as figures, identifiable by the objects in their possession:

Faith is depicted leaning on a cross, holding a candle, or holding a chalice.

Charity tends to have a hand pointing toward her chest or to have her breasts exposed as a sign of maternal nurturing. Other times she is shown carrying food for the poor.

Hope is recognized by the presence of an anchor, ship, or flowers.

Temperance became a very popular symbol during the Prohibition era and can be identified by a water pitcher or sheathed sword.

Justice is one of the most widely recognized virtues because she is always shown holding a scale. She's not typically found in the cemetery except near the graves of lawyers and judges.

Fortitude is a warrior archetype and can be identified by her hand resting on her hip or a sword or club hanging at her side.

Prudence is the least likely of the virtues to be seen in a cemetery, but if you are lucky enough to come across her, she will either have a snake around her arm or be holding a mirror.

Secret societies and fraternal organizations

Secret societies, fraternal organizations, and other clubs have played a big role in forming and influencing societal relationships throughout history. It is only natural that a person's gravestone would contain symbols representing a group they were a part of.

The best-understood type of societal organization is a religious group. Religious iconography is easy to spot and interpret for most people, even if they are not part of a particular faith; the same cannot be said for smaller or more secretive groups.

Below are the five groups whose imagery may be featured on your ancestors' headstones.

It is important to note that the vast majority of these clubs were historically only open to cisgender men.

Freemasons

Though the Masons have been around in one form or another since the sixteenth century, they didn't become the organization we recognize today until 1717. Because of their longevity, there is a wide variety of grave symbols that can be associated with them. The best-known of these images are the square and compass, the capital letter "G," an eye inside a triangle, and the handshake.

Independent Order of Odd Fellows

Like the Masons, the Odd Fellows are an old and well-respected organization in the UK, the USA, and Canada. By the mid-1700s, there were multiple lodges across England, and in the early 1800s the organization reached America. Odd Fellowship is nonpartisan, nonsectarian, and open to all people regardless of religion, race and cultural identity, gender, and sexual orientation. However, until 1843 the organization only allowed white men. The charter was adjusted that year to include African American men, and in 1851, the Odd Fellows opened their doors to women. The most common Odd Fellows headstone symbol is the three-linked chain. The female branch, known as the Daughters of Rebekah, also sometimes uses the three-linked chain, but incorporates a dove into the motif, as well as the capital letter "R."

American Legion and Royal Canadian Legion

The American Legion is a nonprofit organization that serves veterans and encourages patriotism in the USA, and the Royal Canadian Legion is a nonprofit that serves veterans and ex-RCMP (Royal Canadian Mounted Police) officers in Canada. Both groups help design and care for the graves of veterans and have their own distinct emblems and imagery.

The American Legion emblem typically includes the words "American Legion"; a star, which represents victory and honor; and a wreath, which represents the lives lost during service.

The Royal Canadian Legion emblem contains a maple leaf, which is the symbol of Canada; a crown, which represents the monarchy; a poppy, which is a symbol of veterans of World War I and World War II; and the word "Legion." Some Legion graves have just the image of a poppy instead of the full emblem. The poppy has become a symbol for all veterans in Canada, so if you see one it is a good indication that the person served at some point.

Benevolent and Protective Order of Elks

The Benevolent and Protective Order of Elks began as a social club in New York City in 1868 and quickly grew to be one of the most popular fraternal organizations in America. Even today they have over two thousand lodges and groups, some of which are open to women, thanks to a vote in 1995. The Benevolent and Protective Order of Elks grave marker contains the head of an elk, the letters "BPOE," and the Latin name of the species of elk they admire, *Cervus alces*.

Woodmen of the World

The Woodmen of the World (now known as Modern Woodmen of America) is a fraternal organization turned insurance company founded in the late 1800s in Nebraska. One common symbol of the Woodmen in a cemetery is the gravestone itself. During the Victorian era, tree-stump-shaped gravestones became popular, and naturally the Woodmen flocked to these. Other symbols of the Woodmen are axes and logs accompanied by the phrase "Here Lies a Woodman of the World."

Activity: Symbolism scavenger hunt

One fun way to get to know the symbols of the cemetery is to participate in a scavenger hunt. This activity can be done alone or with a friend. Remember to follow all the cemetery safety guidelines—this isn't a race. Don't run, or you risk injuring yourself or someone else.

> TIP: Head to a large city cemetery for the scavenger hunt, as a wider variety of symbols will be available.

Give each person a copy of the following list.

Record what you think each symbol represents.

Be sure to leave a little offering for each spirit whose headstone helps you in this search. Coins or pretty stones are generally appreciated. You can also record the information on each headstone if you'd like to present a more substantial offering later.

1. Wheat
2. Elk/deer
3. Cross
4. Death's-head
5. Butterfly
6. Torch
7. Snake
8. Dog
9. Ivy
10. Sun

Bonus

1. Find a headstone with your birth date.
2. Find a headstone with the same first name as you.
3. Find a headstone with the same last name as you.
4. Find the oldest grave you can.
5. Find the sexton.

RESEARCH MODE

Before you begin your spiritual or magical work with your ancestors in the cemetery, you need to know precisely where they are located.

For many people, the gravestone may be the final piece in their genealogical puzzle, or it could be the only record of someone's existence!

If you're starting from scratch, here are some ways to locate your loved ones.

Ask living relatives

Asking family members is often the quickest and easiest way to figure out where your ancestors are buried. Most of the time, relatives will know the name of the cemetery and who is buried there, but if you're really lucky, they will also know sections and plot numbers.

Utilize online communities

There are three important websites you should have in your research rotation for finding graves. All three provide transcriptions, photos, cemetery locations, and plot numbers.

Find a Grave

The website Findagrave.com is the "world's largest grave site collection." With over 210 million records (and growing each day), this website should be your first stop.

Find a Grave allows you to search for the graves of your ancestors easily by using as much or as little information as you have. They also give you the option of searching specific cemeteries or locations. Not only are they affiliated with Ancestry (Ancestry.com) for easy cross-referencing, but they also have their own forums on the website where you can connect with others doing research.

There is even an app for easy use at the cemetery.

BillionGraves

The website Billiongraves.com also contains millions of records, as well as the world's largest collection of grave site GPS data, which comes in handy for smaller, more rural locations.

The search function on BillionGraves is highly intuitive. You can add or subtract years to your searches in case the written records you have are incorrect (a common problem in genealogy).

Interment.net

The site Interment.net is not as big as the other two, but it is growing every day.

One great feature of this website is that it allows you to search under "special collections," such as train wreck deaths, mining deaths, and even the records of flooded cemeteries!

Interment.net also provides you with name variations in the results in case the spelling is slightly off (another common genealogy problem).

Cemetery and graveyard records

As handy as these three websites can be, they don't have all the cemeteries completely documented or photographed.

Your ancestor may have been buried but was unable to afford a headstone and thus won't always show up online.

If you know what neighborhood your ancestors lived in, check with the cemeteries in a five-to-ten-mile radius.

You can likely narrow down the search parameters if you know your ancestor's religious affiliation or if they lived in a big city.

These days, privately owned cemeteries often keep their records online, but that isn't a guarantee.

The easiest way to find out if your ancestor is buried somewhere is to call the cemetery and ask if they have hard copies of the interment records. Chances are they will look for you or invite you to look yourself.

If you have the opportunity to go in person, definitely do so. Cemetery and graveyard interment records contain lots of valuable information, such as cause of death, purchase receipts, next of kin, plot numbers, and even street addresses.

Other records

Most of the time, you will encounter online records that can lead to a cemetery location, such as obituaries, death certificates, funeral notices, and church registers.

Using gravestones for further research

Make a list of names on nearby gravestones. These may belong to ancestors you haven't identified yet, and they can also reveal the maiden names of your female relatives.

Look for the graves of infants or children who were born and died between censuses.

Gravestones can reveal the cause of death; it is sometimes etched directly on the gravestone.

Pay special attention to dates on surrounding stones. If a woman died the same day as a child was born, or shortly thereafter, her death may have been the result of complications of childbirth.

Multiple graves with the same death date can indicate an accident or natural disaster.

Death dates within a few days or weeks of one another can indicate an illness, pandemic, or war.

What to include in your BOA

For each ancestor, you should include the following information and any documents you have:

Cemetery name:

Section:

Plot number:

Shared or single plot:

Inscription/Epitaph:

Don't forget to include a written description of the grave site and take photos from every angle.

Material:

Shape and style:

Symbols:

Color:

Decorations (trees, plants):

Existing damage:

Documents such as maps, search records, plot deeds, and receipts should also be included.

CHAPTER TEN

PLANNING YOUR DEATH

10

Planning Your Death

Because I could not stop for Death—
He kindly stopped for me—
The Carriage held but just Ourselves—
And Immortality.

—EMILY DICKINSON

PLANNING FOR DEATH

Remember in the BOA chapter when I asked you to designate a section in the back of the book that we would work on later? Well, it is now that time.

It was important to me that this be the last chapter of the book. Working on your own death is symbolic of the journey you have taken from beginning your ancestor practice to now.

When it comes to end-of-life planning, most of us drag our feet. We tend to think we have all the time in the world or that we are somehow the exception to the rule that says one day we will die.

But we will.

One day, we will be ancestors in someone's veneration practice.

While my wish is that we all have long and healthy lives, it is still important that we prepare for the day when that time comes.

So why is end-of-life planning important?

For starters, it helps ease the burden on our loved ones. The last thing they will need while grieving is the responsibility of having to decide on the arrangements for our funeral and burial, all while figuring out how to pay for everything.

One of the best gifts you can offer your loved ones is to have some sort of plan in place.

Think about all the research and work you have done putting together your BOA. Now imagine if your ancestors had each handed you a section about themselves, completely filled in. By including this section about yourself, you are essentially giving that gift to your descendants.

Not only will they learn the practical facts about you, but they will also receive instructions on how to ritualistically work with your spirit.

I will be using myself as an example in this chapter to give you an idea of what is needed.

While this process can be difficult, you should try to make the most of it. Imagine how much comfort this will bring to your family one day.

EXPENSES

The first thing you should do before filling out the following prompts is to open a savings account and set up a weekly or monthly deposit to go toward all death expenses. Decide what is appropriate based on any other funds your family will receive upon your death, such as from insurance or the government.

Even if you feel like you can't save a significant amount right now, just know that anything in this account will be helpful to your loved ones when they are making your arrangements.

LEGAL COMPONENTS

There is a lot of paperwork when it comes to dying. Forms will need to be filled out, death certificates will need to be paid for, and various bank and utility accounts will have to be closed.

Laws surrounding wills and estates vary from country to country and even state to state, so it is important that you understand what you need to do before you die. Take the pressure off your family by organizing the following for them (with a lawyer):

- Your last will and testament
- Your assignment of an estate executor
- A list of all your assets
- A list of your debts
- Insurance information
- Banking information
- A health care proxy (this document appoints a person who can make your medical decisions if you are incapacitated)
- A power of attorney

DO THE CENSUS...ON YOURSELF

Once you have all the legal components straightened out, it's time to provide your descendants with any information they will need to know about who you are.

Remember in chapter 6 when we looked at examples of census questions? Take some of those as prompts and fill them in about yourself.

> TIP: Use "Enlist the Living" on pages 112–14 for ideas about what else you can include for a more rounded personality profile of yourself.

PHOTOS

To accompany your basic information, you may wish to include a series of photos of yourself. I recommend choosing one for every five years of your life so your descendants can see your progression from newborn to adult.

You can also pick specific milestones to include, such as weddings and graduations.

Did you know that for some people, the only photo ever taken of them was snapped after they died? In the nineteenth century, the advent of photography meant that people had the ability to document their lives in a new way. Because of the high mortality rate at the time, people began taking family portraits with their deceased loved ones as mementos.

FUNERAL AND BURIAL

One of the most essential parts of death planning is knowing what type of funeral and burial you would like to have.

I recommend drafting two plans: one with a low budget and one with a high budget. Then make a point of contributing to your savings account monthly.

Don't forget to make sure your plan is realistic! If your dream is to have your ashes scattered at the foot of the Great Pyramid in Egypt, then you need to work out what steps that would entail and how to pay for them.

Answer questions like "How much would airfare be?" and "What sorts of permits are needed?"

You don't want the feeling of guilt to be the legacy you leave behind for your loved ones because they were unable to fulfill your request (or resentment if they extend beyond their means to accommodate you!), so always, always, always have a backup plan. At the very least, you should leave a note that states that you'll be happy so long as they try their best.

Making a funeral plan

- What sort of funeral do you want?
- Will it be religious or secular?
- What sort of tone will it have? Solemn, celebratory, etc.?
- Will it include flowers?
- Will there be funeral stationery?
- How many guests will be invited?
- Who will be in charge of organizing it?
- Will there be a visitation or wake?
- Will there be a reception?

MY BURIAL ARRANGEMENT

Headstone, Urn and Casket Wishlist

CLAIRE GOODCHILD
FEB 13TH 1988
DEATH

GOODCHILD

- Will you be embalmed for the visitation and funeral?
- What style of casket or coffin do you prefer?
- Will you be cremated?

Once you have the specifics straightened out, make a list of your top three funeral parlor choices.

My high-budget funeral

I would like a witchy, gothic-style funeral that mixes mourning and celebration.

I would like white roses to be arranged around my casket and the rest of the room.

My casket should be a dark wood with a light interior and silver hardware. If I am presentable, it should be an open-casket funeral.

> TIP: Decide now what type of outfit you want to be buried in!

I want the classic funeral elements, such as the funeral parlor service, visitation, and a catered reception.

I would also like to have some tarot readers at the wake to pass along any last messages or advice I have for the living in a fun way. Tarot represents a major part of my life's work, and I would love for it to be part of my send-off.

My low-budget funeral

Again, a witchy vibe for the service, but the mourning rituals can be limited to a small funeral and a wake at a restaurant.

I would still love white roses to be a theme, but perhaps they can be limited to one centerpiece and a few vases on tables.

Instead of an open-casket service, I can do "direct to cremation" and be in a nice silver or emerald urn on a table with roses.

Instead of tarot readers, each guest, on their way out, may be given a tarot card from one of the decks I designed.

BURIAL PLANS

Another major decision to be made is what sort of burial you would like. As you can see from my funeral plan, my budget options determine which route I take.

As with the funeral planning, you need to decide on your top three cemeteries or graveyards. I have high hopes of being buried alongside my paternal family, but costs are already in the tens of thousands due to limited space.

You also need to figure out whether your funeral parlor does cremation or whether your body will need to be transported to a different location first. As cities and towns will change over time, it is important to keep this part of your plan updated regularly.

High-budget burial plan

I wish to be buried in Prospect Cemetery in Toronto, in either section 11 or section 12, near my ancestors.

I would like a flat, dark-granite headstone engraved with my name, birth date, death date, and a tarot spread I have designed so that people can visit my grave and ask questions with their cards.

Low-budget burial plan

I am happy to be cremated, but I would still like for my urn to be buried in a cremation plot in Prospect Cemetery in Toronto with my tarot-themed headstone.

Ultra-low-budget burial plan

I am happy to be cremated and have my cremains passed among family members every few years. Or to have my cremains divided into small urns and given to each of my closest descendants.

I would like my urn (or urns) to be a simple silver or emerald-green color.

CHOOSING A HEADSTONE

These days, many headstone companies have a cost calculator built right into their websites so you can figure out what sort of price you will be looking at down the road. By revisiting this part of your plan every few years, you're making sure that prices are always reflected accurately for your loved ones.

You can determine stone, finish, style, and custom engraving with a few clicks of your mouse.

Remember in chapter 9 where I asked you to design a mini-headstone for a loved one? Now try designing one for yourself! Use the dictionary in that chapter to help you decide on symbols and styles that are right for you.

Choosing an urn

Like headstones, urns are more customizable than ever. You can order an engraved urn ahead of time online and not worry about price markups from the funeral home.

You can determine metal, finish, style, and custom engraving with a few clicks of your mouse.

RITUAL INFORMATION

Arguably, the rituals you want performed in your honor are the most important element to include in this section of your BOA. Ritual is an essential component of ancestor work. With your ancestors, you have had to experiment with different methods and offerings to see what works best. By telling your loved ones what you would prefer, you can save them a lot of time and effort.

Fill in the following prompts. Use my examples to help you.

Favorite food offering: salt-and-vinegar chips

Favorite drink offering: English breakfast tea

Favorite flower or herb: rose, thistle

Favorite colors: green, black, and white

Favorite scent: vanilla

Favorite book: *Wuthering Heights*

BURBANK MONUMENT CO.

No. 1 Harp, 3½x6 in.
No. 2 " 3x5 in.
No. 3 " 7x12 in.

No. 1 Golden Sheaf, 3x4½ in.
No. 2 " " 4⅜x6 in.
No. 4 " " 9x11½ in.

No. 2 Crown, 5½x2⅜ in.
No. 4 " 4x1⅞ in.
No. 5 " 8x3½ in.

No. 1 Hand, 4½x6 in.
No. 2 " 3½x5 in.
No. 3 " 7½x10¼ in.
No. 4 " 5x7⅞ in.

No. 1 Hour Glass and Scythe, 4x5 in.
No. 1 Hour Glass, 4x3 in.
No. 2 " " 6½x4½ in.
No. 2 Hour Glass and Scythe, 5½x8½ in.

No. 1 Cross and Crown 4x4½ in.
No. 3 " " " 6x8½ in.
No. 4 " " " 4¼x6½ in.
No. 6 " " " 7½x12 in.

No. 2 Dove, 5x5½ in.
No. 3 " 3⅜x2½ in.
No. 4 " 7x8 in.

Favorite music: folk

Favorite movie: *Eternal Sunshine of the Spotless Mind*

Languages: English; some Spanish, Slovakian, and Greek

How to communicate: cartomancy (tarot and oracle decks)

How often to be contacted: daily

Area of expertise: career, witchcraft

Archetype: unknown

LETTER TO DESCENDANTS

The final task is to write a letter to your descendants.

While I can't tell you what to write for this part, I do have some suggestions you may find useful:

- What you hope they will get out of ancestor work
- Why you started this journey with ancestor work
- What you got out of ancestor work
- What you have enjoyed about your life
- What you would change if you could
- Advice for situations such as work, marriage, and child-rearing
- Any last wishes or requests
- Spells and rituals you would like performed in your honor

For my descendants,

My wish is that you all live long and
healthy lives filled with joy and excitement.

Housed on this letter are my final wishes,
along with instructions on how I would like
to be communicated with and honored
your practice.

I understand that it may be hard to read.
Just know that I am here with you every
step of the way.

~ Claire

ACKNOWLEDGMENTS

Meg, Emma, and everyone at Voracious: I can never thank you enough for creating this book with me.

Codi, Adalinh, and Majorie: Thank you for the wonderful and insightful words. Your contributions will help so many people.

I would also like to thank Wellcome Collection, Rawpixel, and all other libraries and museums that have collected antique texts and made them available to the public copyright-free. This has enabled me to create the artistic collages and digital art that appear in this book.

RESOURCES

Resources on Black and Indigenous ancestors

African Ancestry https://africanancestry.com

Afro-American Historical and Genealogical Society
https://www.aahgs.org

Association on American Indian Affairs (USA)
https://www.indian-affairs.org

Black Cemetery Network https://blackcemeterynetwork.org

Digital Library on American Slavery http://dlas.uncg.edu

Enslaved: Peoples of the Historical Slave Trade https://enslaved.org

Freedmen's Bureau Project https://www.archives.gov/research/african-americans/freedmens-bureau

International African American Museum Center for Family History
https://cfh.iaamuseum.org

Library and Archives Canada—Indigenous Genealogy https://www.bac-lac.gc.ca/eng/discover/aboriginal-heritage/Pages/genealogy.aspx

National Centre for Truth and Reconciliation (Canada) https://nctr.ca

TIP: Many genealogical websites and archives, such as Ancestry.com, contain Black- and Indigenous-specific search guides.

DNA resources

African Ancestry https://africanancestry.com

Ancestry https://www.ancestry.com

FamilyTreeDNA https://www.familytreedna.com

GEDmatch https://www.gedmatch.com

MyHeritage https://www.myheritage.com

23andMe https://www.23andme.com

Cemetery resources

BillionGraves https://billiongraves.com

Black Cemetery Network https://blackcemeterynetwork.org

Find a Grave https://www.findagrave.com

Interment.net http://www.interment.net/Default.htm

Names In Stone https://www.namesinstone.com

Genealogical records resources

AccessGenealogy https://accessgenealogy.com

Ancestry https://www.ancestry.com

FamilySearch https://www.familysearch.org/en/

Findmypast https://www.findmypast.com

Genealogy Trails http://genealogytrails.com

HeritageQuest Online https://about.proquest.com/en/products-services/
HeritageQuest-Online/

Library and Archives Canada https://www.bac-lac.gc.ca/eng/Pages/home.aspx

Library of Congress https://www.loc.gov

National Archives and Records Administration https://www.archives.gov

Newspapers

British Newspaper Archive https://www.britishnewspaperarchive.co.uk

Chronicling America https://chroniclingamerica.loc.gov

NewspaperArchive https://newspaperarchive.com

TIP: Your local library may have many newspapers archived and available online.

CORRESPONDENCES

Plants of the dead

See "Flora: plants of the dead" in chapter 9, "A Guide to Cemeteries."

Color correspondences

Color can and should be incorporated in your rituals. It is one of the easiest ways to add energy to your spells.

White and black: death, spirits, protection, mystery, power, peace, wisdom, magic, spirituality

Gold and silver: wealth, luck, enhancement, luxury, solar and lunar energy

Brown: earth, grounding, stability, home, strength

Green: luck, prosperity, health, wealth, nature, success, growth, greed

Blue: calmness, tranquility, depression, communication, emotions, intuition, negativity

Red: bloodline, lineage, passion, love, anger, aggression, life, ambition

Pink: care, comfort, beauty, compassion, love

Purple: psychic ability, royalty, knowledge, spirituality, the divine

Orange: energy, courage, determination, creativity

Yellow: happiness, joy, playfulness, clarity, positivity, friendship, infidelity

Astrological associations

To create a full astrological chart for a person, you need to know their birth time, but knowing their sun sign (zodiac sign) can give you a little glimpse into part of their personality. This can help you to tailor your rituals.

Note: People born on a "cusp" day, when the sun moves from one sign to another, are not "both signs." A person is always either one zodiac sign or the other, and in order to know which you will need a birth time.

Some of the dates for the zodiac signs vary year to year, so the following list is an approximation. You can use an astrological ephemeris to see on which day a sign starts or ends in any particular year.

Aries

Symbol: the ram
Dates: March 21 to April 20
Planetary ruler: Mars
Element: fire
Keywords: determined, natural leader, independent, brash, egotistical

Taurus

Symbol: the bull
Dates: April 21 to May 20
Planetary ruler: Venus
Element: earth
Keywords: stubborn, methodical, generous, artistic, overindulgent

Gemini

Symbol: the twins
Dates: May 21 to June 20
Planetary ruler: Mercury
Element: air
Keywords: adaptable, impatient, inquisitive, mischievous, intellectual

Cancer

Symbol: the crab
Dates: June 21 to July 21
Planetary ruler: the moon
Element: water
Keywords: sensitive, nurturing, defensive, vulnerable, receptive

Leo

Symbol: the lion
Dates: July 22 to August 22
Planetary ruler: the sun
Element: fire
Keywords: prideful, egotistical, ambitious, loyal, confident, creative

Virgo

Symbol: the virgin
Dates: August 23 to September 22
Planetary ruler: Mercury
Element: earth
Keywords: supportive, innovative, analytical, biting, repressed

Libra

Symbol: the scales
Dates: September 23 to October 22
Planetary ruler: Venus
Element: air
Keywords: diplomatic, flirty, petty, inquisitive, arrogant

Scorpio

Symbol: the scorpion
Dates: October 23 to November 21
Planetary rulers: Mars and Pluto

Element: water
Keywords: transformative, mysterious, calculating, vengeful, passionate

Sagittarius

Symbol: the archer
Dates: November 22 to December 20
Planetary ruler: Jupiter
Element: fire
Keywords: optimistic, adaptable, irritable, impatient, exuberant

Capricorn

Symbol: the goat
Dates: December 21 to January 20
Planetary ruler: Saturn
Element: earth
Keywords: resourceful, determined, callous, insecure, logical

Aquarius

Symbol: the water bearer
Dates: January 21 to February 18
Planetary rulers: Saturn and Uranus
Element: air
Keywords: inventive, humanitarian, future-oriented, rebellious, temperamental

Pisces

Symbol: the fish
Dates: February 19 to March 20
Planetary rulers: Jupiter and Neptune
Element: water
Keywords: graceful, mystical, dreamy, overly sensitive, selfish

Days of the week

Zodiac signs aren't the only way to incorporate celestial energy into your workings. The days of the week and phases of the moon can also be harnessed for their spiritual benefits.

Monday

Ruled by the moon.
Best day for dealing with ancestral trauma and emotional matters.

Tuesday

Ruled by Mars.
Best day for protection rituals and spells. Also a great day for working with the archetypes.

Wednesday

Ruled by Mercury.
Best day for communication or performing divination with spirits.

Thursday

Ruled by Jupiter.
Best day for matters relating to career or finances. Also a positive day for doing ancestor research.

Friday

Ruled by Venus.
Best day for connecting with newly discovered ancestors or building existing relationships.

Saturday

Ruled by Saturn.
Best day for doing research or working on your BOA.

Sunday

Ruled by the sun.
Best day for any sort of ritual or spell because of its auspicious nature.

Moon phases

New moon

The new moon is all about beginnings and fresh starts. This is the best time to embark on a new spiritual practice or approach ancestors you don't have an existing relationship with.

Waxing moon

As the moon grows, so does the energy that surrounds us. The waxing moon expands our hearts and minds, which allows us to be more receptive to messages and signs from our ancestors.

Full moon

The full moon illuminates everything hidden in the shadows. This phase can be utilized for fast and intense results. It is the perfect time for any sort of ritual or offering for your ancestors.

Waning moon

As the light of the moon diminishes, so do our fears and resentments. The waning moon is a great time for releasing grief.

Wheel of the Year

The Wheel of the Year is a calendar that is made up of eight Sabbats, or "holidays." They take place roughly around the same date each year. Witches of all paths can and do celebrate these festivals.

Four of the Sabbats take place on the four solar days of the year (summer solstice, fall equinox, winter solstice, and spring equinox), and the remaining four Sabbats take place at the midpoint between these solar events.

Because of their spiritual significance, these dates are perfect for honoring and working with your ancestors.

Because the dates can change year to year, these are just approximations.

Imbolc

Northern Hemisphere: February 1 to 2
Southern Hemisphere: August 1 to 2

Imbolc is the Sabbat that falls between Yule (winter solstice) and Ostara (spring equinox). Imbolc represents the first stirring or awakening of the coming spring. While we may not see the obvious signs of spring until much later, this Sabbat reminds us that the wheels are in motion.

Ostara

Northern Hemisphere: March 19 to 23
Southern Hemisphere: September 19 to 23

Ostara is the Sabbat that honors the spring equinox. The days and nights are of equal length, and warmth is beginning to come back into our lives. Ostara revolves around rebirth, renewal, and fertility. Ostara is an amalgamation of different festivals and holidays from the pagan world that were joined together in the twentieth century, and is celebrated mostly by modern Wiccans.

Beltane

Northern Hemisphere: April 30 to May 1
Southern Hemisphere: October 31 to November 1

Beltane falls between the spring equinox and the summer solstice. Beltane is a fire festival that honors summer's imminent arrival. This Sabbat is mainly about fertility, purification, and protection.

Litha

Northern Hemisphere: June 19 to 23
Southern Hemisphere: December 19 to 23

The Sabbat Litha falls on the summer solstice and is all about giving thanks for the sun and all it provides for us. The days are now much longer than the nights. Fresh vegetables, herbs, and flowers are gathered during the day, and at night bonfires are lit in honor of the sun. After Litha ends, the days begin to get shorter.

Lughnasadh or Lammas

Northern Hemisphere: August 1 to 2
Southern Hemisphere: February 1 to 2

Lughnasadh is the first Sabbat of the harvest season and takes place between the summer solstice and the autumn equinox. While the days are still long and hot, signs of autumn are beginning to creep into the environment. The first of the crops are ready to be harvested, and preparations begin for the season of darkness.

Mabon

Northern Hemisphere: September 20 to 24
Southern Hemisphere: March 20 to 24

Mabon takes place on the autumn equinox and is very much like the witches' Thanksgiving. The day and night are once again of equal lengths, and more and more foods are ready to be harvested and preserved. Rituals are focused around saying goodbye to the sun.

Samhain

Northern Hemisphere: October 31 to November 1
Southern Hemisphere: April 30 to May 1

Samhain is the Sabbat between the autumn equinox and the winter solstice. For many people this celebration is known as Halloween. Samhain is the time of year when ancestors and spirits receive the most attention, as it is believed the veil between our world and their world is at its thinnest.

Yule

Northern Hemisphere: December 19 to 23
Southern Hemisphere: June 19 to 23

Yule takes place on the winter solstice and therefore during the longest night of the year. Many modern Christmas traditions come from Yule. This Sabbat is all about community and making plans for the upcoming year, as after Yule the days once again grow longer.

Gemstones

Gemstones and minerals can have their own energies that can be incorporated into rituals. They also make beautiful offerings, but it is important to do your research about where they are mined to ensure that the mining company isn't violating human rights.

Rose quartz: love, beauty, comfort

Clear quartz: manifesting, divination, cleansing

Black tourmaline: grounding, protection, banishing

Amethyst: clairvoyance, psychic ability, mental clarity

Citrine: money, abundance, creativity

Aventurine: confidence, luck, abundance

Cyanite: removing negativity; connection, dreams

Pyrite: money, inspiration, protection

Bloodstone: building connections; balance, improving memory

Obsidian: protection, spiritual growth, absorbing negativity

Incense

Smell is one of our most powerful senses in terms of evoking memories and bringing up different emotions—for us, and for the spirits.

Cedar: purification, psychic powers, success

Frankincense: psychic protection, strength, perseverance

Rosemary: home protection, spiritual cleansing, creativity, sensitivity

Pine: general protection, healing, longevity

Cinnamon: love, passion, power, career

Rose: love, beauty, compassion, innocence

Clove: removing negativity, restoring balance, money

Lavender: relaxation, serenity, happiness, dreams

Patchouli: focus, meditation, cleansing, balance

Sandalwood: general protection, persistence, purification, spiritual cleansing

Lemongrass: removing negativity; mental clarity, focus, admiration

Juniper: removing hexes; home and spiritual protection

Vanilla: love, friendship, family, ancestors

Lily: mourning, forgiveness, tranquility

GLOSSARY

Altar: A sacred space that is used for ritual purposes and honoring ancestors.

Ancestors: The people from whom you are descended on a genetic or spiritual level.

Ancestor veneration: The practice of honoring your ancestors in a spiritual or magical way.

Cemetery: A plot of land designated for burying the dead that is either government-run or privately owned, and open to everyone regardless of ethnicity, gender, or faith.

Divination: The act of interpreting signs and symbols in order to communicate with spirits or gain knowledge about the unknown.

DNA: Deoxyribonucleic acid, the material responsible for the function of a living thing. DNA is inherited, or passed down by your ancestors.

Family history book: A book containing a person's family history, or stories relating to their ancestors.

Family tree: A chart or diagram that shows the genetic (or spiritual) relationships among a group of people.

Ghost: The physical manifestation of a deceased person.

Graveyard: A plot of land designated for burying the dead. Graveyards are usually rural, and attached to a specific religion.

Grimoire: A book used by witches and occultists that contains mystical knowledge.

Heirloom: An item of monetary value that has been passed down through a family for generations.

Intelligent haunting: An intentional interaction between the spirit of a deceased person and a living person (or environment).

Keepsake: An item that has sentimental value that is passed down through a family for generations.

Offerings: Gifts and ritual items given to ancestors and spirits.

Paranormal: Phenomena associated with ghosts and spirits that cannot be explained by current scientific methods.

Physical realm: The realm or plane of existence in which the physical world is located.

Red thread: The genetic bloodline shared by family members, or a metaphorical bloodline that connects people spiritually.

Residual haunting: An energetic imprint of a ghost on an environment.

Ritual: A series of actions that can include spells, movements, or other activities, intended to either honor something or someone or achieve some desired outcome.

Séance: A session at which a person or group of people attempts to communicate with the dead.

Sigil: A drawing or symbol that contains magical energy.

Spell: A word or phrase, either spoken or written, that is thought to grant the caster some desired outcome.

Spirit: The animating force of all things, alive, dead, and supernatural.

Spirit realm: The realm or plane of existence in which the spirit world is located.

Spiritualism: A religious movement that focused on spirit communication in the 1800s and early 1900s.

DEATH

THREE OF SWORDS

ABOUT THE AUTHOR

Claire Goodchild is an award-winning artist, photographer, designer, and writer from Toronto. She created the wildly popular tarot deck the Antique Anatomy Tarot, which features antique medical images, and she was the first person to create an astrology-themed oracle deck, the Arcana of Astrology. She is also the author of *The Book of Séances*.